VICTIM TO VICTORY

Change Starts with Your Story

PRODUCED BY TRACEY COOK

Edited by Lil Barcaski and Linda Hinkle

Published by: GWN Publishing
www.GWNPublishing.com

Cover Design: Kristina Conatser Captured by KC Design

ISBN: 979-8-9867817-6-1

FOREWORD

by *Mary Kate O'Connell*

I've known Tracey Cook since early 2019 and met several of the individuals she asked to bravely share their stories in the pages of this book. Knowing the depths and struggles from which they've triumphantly emerged, each with a new calling in life, makes me proud – and fortunate to call them friends. If you've ever struggled to find hope and purpose, this book is for you.

The Tracey I first knew was smart and talented, but fearful of how others perceived her – believing that people in her life talked around her, and not to her. To see her step into her power and discover her purpose, has been to watch a total transformation that I know Tracey herself would hardly think possible just three short years ago. Today, she's an entrepreneur, a coach, a mentor, and most of all, a champion for the voiceless and victimized. Tracey has a passion that's difficult to quantify, but it's tireless and unwavering, and evident in the work she does every day to lead others from victimhood to victory.

Victim to Victory shows us what's possible, regardless of the circumstances we may find ourselves in, at any given time. It's about the human spirit, our desire to heal and grow, to press on and get the ship righted. To conquer the darkness. This wonderful compilation gives us a glimpse, up close, of the vulnerabilities of each author and the strength of their determination.

The things that wound us don't have to hold us back forever. We have a say in that matter. When we let something go, it doesn't mean it never happened or didn't hurt us deeply. But it enables us to fight on and eventually come out the other side. That's a powerful lesson for anyone who is in the throes of a difficult situation or conflict. Sometimes, just knowing you can get through it, is enough to get you moving again. This book gives us all hope and courage to carry forward.

T.D. Jakes once said, "When you hold on to your history, you do it at the expense of your destiny." You will see the power of those words ring true in every chapter of this book. Separate lives, a spectrum of different kinds of challenges – but all linked by each author's embrace of a new freedom. And it's clearly something they want their readers to experience as well.

Let these stories bring you hope. Allow them to move you and make you think. And honestly ask yourself if there's a part of you in each of them. Most of all, let them inspire you to make changes you need to make to find a new path of freedom and happiness. We all deserve that, despite what's been thrown at us by life. These authors show you how they achieved their freedom. I hope this book helps many others find theirs.

One of the greatest gifts I receive as a coach is hearing a client say, "You believed in me before I believed in myself." Believing in others is simple for me because I know we're all children of God, worthy of love because we are here.

My thanks and love to Tracey for shining her light in this world, that sometimes feels overwhelmingly dark and hopeless. Thank you for sharing your journey with me over the past few years. I'm immensely proud of you, and blessed to have you in my corner. Thank you for never giving up and being a beacon of light for everyone whose life will change by discovering these stories.

Mary Kate O'Connell is an author, mindset coach, entrepreneur, and co-founder of the Intentional Living Room, a community where members are challenged to take charge of their lives and become the driver instead of the passenger. Members are uplifted and encouraged to step into their greatness and create the life they desire through mindset work, support, encouragement, virtual hugs, and real talk without judgment.

IntentionalLivingRoom.com

ENDORSEMENTS

An extraordinary book filled with stories of powerful women and men who are powerhouses. If you need inspiration, look no further than this book. It will uplift you, motivate you and arm you with the knowledge that you can face adversity, overcome it, and still win.

Elsa Morgan
Founder and CEO at Elsa Morgan – The Queenie Effect Pty Ltd
https://elsamorgan.com/

I've seen how stories impact first hand, this book is a powerful guide to help you navigate the challenges in life. This book is all you need to change your world and others too.

Stacey Hall
Stacey Hall, #1 Best-Selling Author, 'Selling From Your Comfort Zone'
https://www.staceyannhall.com/home

CONTENTS

TRACEY COOK

*To my Family: By sharing my story I hope to
break generational abuse cycles and leave a
legacy of love and abundance for generations to
come.*

THE STEEP CLIMB TO VICTORY

by *Tracey Cook*

I opened my eyes, laying on a bed of a hospital room. The doctors and nurses felt like they were moving slowly around me. My arms were hooked up to machines that were beeping. My body felt heavy, stiff, and sore. My breathing was shallow and my heart was beating faster and harder than I had ever felt it before. Suddenly, the lights dimmed. I looked down at my body and all I could see were bruises and cuts. My large, heavily 8-month pregnant, belly was covered in bruises. I started to cry with moans of pains, with muffled words that nobody could understand, not even myself.

The doctors were talking and I could not understand a word they were saying and the Chaplain was talking to me about God. Then I clearly heard the words, "Your baby isn't going to survive, you need to prepare yourself!"

That's when all went silent. I had never been so calm. That's when the previous few hours of abuse came flooding into my thoughts. I had been at home, cleaning and cooking. My partner at the time was out with his friends drinking once again. It was early evening, and my baby was kicking and moving a lot, so I went and laid down on the bed for a rest. I was home alone and was starting to panic because my stomach was hurting. I called my partner and told him to come home. I was scared, this was my first baby, and being eight months pregnant, I didn't really know what to expect.

A few hours later, he arrived back home, very drunk, verbally abusing me saying that I had ruined his night out and that I should have just gone to the hospital if I was that worried. I was crying, worried, and emotional. I shouted at him, I swore at him, and before I realized it, I was running down the hallway being hit by a baseball bat. I was panicked. This was not the first time I had been hit, abused, and emotionally been beaten. I should have never let it get to this point. I felt shame and disgust in myself that I got myself, and now my baby, into this situation.

I had lived a lifetime growing up of being told, "You are a waste of space." "You will never amount to anything." "You're an idiot." "You're not smart enough to do that." "Just shut up and do what you are told."

I grew up in a somewhat traditional family. Dad worked. Mum stayed at home. My father was a very angry man, an alcoholic, and Mum seemed to be very submissive and at times co-dependent. Dad would drink, come home, and be abusive . Mum tried her best to keep things "normal." But I knew, at an early age, that sitting in a room protecting my little brother while Mum and Dad were fighting in the other room was far from normal. I was always on egg shells. Nothing was ever good enough.

In the times good times, we would have family friends come and visit with us from the country. They had two boys and we used to play outside while the parents would play board games inside.

It was fun. Until one day, the oldest boy of the family made me play a game with him that would lead to years of sexual abuse by him on every single visit. I started to wet my bed and tried everything I could to get someone's attention in any way I could. I felt very lonely all of the time. I felt like no one saw me or cared. Every time I wet my bed or couldn't go to sleep in my bed, my parents would smack me, yell at me, threaten me, and even tie me in my bed. One time, they even threw me outside in the middle of the night, telling me that the orphanage was on their way to pick me up because I was so bad. This made me angry, scared, and feeling worthless.

A neighbour heard my cries and my parents had no choice but to drag me back inside. From that night on, I kept all my feelings to myself. I started to be naughty, I was rebellious and never would I again feel like I was part of my family. It was me, on my own. I was in survival mode.

In my teenage years, I was popular at school and had many friends. My outgoing personality seemed to disguise how much I was hurting underneath. I would sneak out and hang around with the "wrong crowd." We would drink, and lie, and hang out with older boys. At the age of 13 and 14, I was going to night clubs, hanging out in biker bars, and I finally felt accepted in a culture where everyone seemed broken too, and that was acceptable. Weekends would be filled with drugs and parties and sitting on the back of Harleys. I finally felt free and accepted.

I ran away from home at 16, lived with a much older boyfriend, and totally self-sabotaged the relationship. I felt lost again, and travelled around Australia, from town to town, relationship to relationship. Always feeling lost and unworthy. Always in abusive relationships, because that's what I thought I deserved.

I had grand plans with a friend to travel to England. The next big adventure. We had four weeks before leaving and we were partying up before we flew out. For me, I had plan never to return to Australia. In this party mode, I met this guy. He was unlike anyone I had ever met. He was kind and caring and we would just talk for hours. I admitted that we could hang out together for a few weeks, but my plans were to fly out soon, never to return. During these few weeks, our relationship grew and I told my friend to go to the UK alone. I was staying here. I was pregnant!

I call this a sliding door moment. This could go either way. I was not ready for this. Maybe this is where I changed my life around. I had to give it a shot. We bought a house. Things were ok for a short while. Then the drinking continued, the abuse continued, and all those limiting beliefs and feelings of disgust in myself came true. I felt trapped.

Like my Mother before me, I was trying to make things work. That's when it escalated to laying in that hospital bed, with the Doctors telling me that I was going to lose my baby!

In that very moment, I declared to myself that if my baby lived, I would no longer allow myself to be abused. I would make a better life, no matter what it took, and once I could do that, I would help others do the same. My daughter is now 28 with 3 children of her own. After 35 years of healing, I now embrace my story, let people know they are seen and worthy, and give them the helping hand up that I always needed.

We just need to be kinder to change the world.

www.traceyleecook.com

Tracey Cook

ALISON LEITHEISER

To my brilliant & devoted family, I am wholeheartedly grateful for you.

QUADRIPLEGIC TO DANCING

by *Alison Leitheiser*

My friends were picking out prom dresses, and I was suddenly paralyzed from the neck down. A rare virus had infiltrated my spinal cord. Over the period of a few months, I started falling. Soon after, I needed help walking and even sitting up. Eventually, I couldn't brush my teeth or use the restroom by myself. I was completely paralyzed from the neck down and yet, I was in constant, excruciating pain. The virus caused me to have seizures, organ damage and severely damaged my nervous system. I went from a straight A student athlete to someone who could no longer move. Countless doctors and specialists couldn't identify what was wrong with me, so they then assumed it must be psychiatric. Teenage girl? She must really be dying for attention.

Through this time of immense suffering, I found strength in my supportive family and my deep relationship with God. Even though I felt confused, overwhelmed, afraid and in constant pain, those two pillars sustained me. I loved listening to Christian music. It was uplifting and changed my perspective from my own difficulties to focusing on something greater than myself.

I would get lost in the darkness of my pain and dizziness. It felt like I was continuously falling. It was comforting when someone would come lay next to me. I cognitively understood they were not falling, which helped me feel more stable. My brother would often drive seven hours just to lay next to me. He spent time reading the Harry Potter books aloud to me. My sisters also came to visit, driving a far distance to help in any way, even shaving my legs. Their generosity and kindness was a lifeline.

As part of our continuous search for answers, I went to an intensive in-patient rehab facility to try to achieve more function. One of my cherished victories while I was there was finally making it through a cafeteria meal while sitting up. I worked toward that goal for weeks. My nervous system was so damaged and hypersensitive that anything more than a whisper caused me stabbing pain. The conversations in the cafeteria, the clinking of silverware, the exhaustion that came from engaging all the muscles needed to hold me upright, and the mechanics of chewing and swallowing seemed as possible as climbing Mt. Everest. When I finally made it through my first meal sitting up, I felt invincible. Making progress, however seemingly small, felt incredible.

During my illness, my mom was my main caretaker. I dreamed of ways to show my gratitude. As a surprise gift, I set a goal of walking by her next birthday. My athletic spirit latched onto that goal, and I worked tirelessly to get there. On her birthday, they brought me out to her in a wheelchair and helped me stand. I wobbled and took my first couple of steps before literally falling into her arms. We laughed. We cried. We celebrated.

However wonderful, achieving my goal came with major consequences. Medicating my symptoms and pushing myself to the limit did not actually repair the damage to my nervous system. Soon after my first steps, I relapsed, and most of my symptoms returned. I was exhausted and discouraged. I retained some limited motion and energy.*

About a year later, we flew to a clinic out of state called Integrative Manual Therapy (IMT). After evaluating me, they said they could actually help us. Tears ran down our cheeks with relief. We did everything they told us: supplements, diet changes, and countless hours of rehab. I began to get better quickly. There were still ups and downs, but the progress was real. Within five months, I was walking several steps at a time without even using a cane. The pain and the organ and nervous system damage took much longer to resolve, but I continued to make progress. IMT helped me heal the root causes, not just medicate the symptoms. I finally found the transformation and hope I had desperately longed for.

Years later, I wanted to give that same hope and gift of transformation to others. I began training at the Center for Integrative Manual Therapy and took all the classes I could. After years of hard work, I was suddenly a therapist. Instead of needing help, I was helping others heal. What a beautiful exchange.

The Bible talks about God's promise to exchange joy for mourning and beauty for ashes. I experienced this in my own story. While I was still sick in the rehab hospital and unable to walk, my sister gave me a pair of Converse® shoes. Years later, those same shoes became my swing dancing shoes!

As a way to show my gratitude to God for my healing, I decided to walk the Camino De Santiago on a 550 miles backpacking pilgrimage with my best friend, Grant. We started our Camino journey on June 17, 2005. One year later, on June 17, 2006, we were married. We took our first steps on our pilgrimage and in marriage on the exact anniversary of my first steps six years earlier on my mom's birthday, June 17, 2000.

Over the years, I continued to experience ups and downs in my healing journey. I had the opportunity to compete for two seasons on American Ninja Warrior. I loved being an athlete again, but I would often push myself too hard. I experienced several setbacks and even ended up in a wheelchair again for a time. In my enthusiasm for life, I often ignored my body's smaller whispers asking for support until it finally had to scream for help. I had to change the way I thought about my body's needs. I decided to think about my body like a bank account. I could not spend all my body's cash at one time and allow myself to become bankrupt. I needed to accurately measure out my withdrawals and balance it with deposits over time.

Healing can be a slow process. I tried all kinds of diets, supplements, machines, and a decade of trauma psychotherapy, but I was still experiencing setbacks. I had supported the structure of my spinal cord, but had not worked on the perceptions and subsequent signals that my brain was making about its environment. The brain is hard wired for survival, and mine was still interpreting elements of my daily life as huge stressors for my body. I wanted more for myself and for my clients. I wanted to find the most effective treatments possible. While practicing the same Integrative Manual Therapy that helped me walk again, I continued to learn about how the brain interprets stress and stores it in the body. Learning this has been a game changer in my life and the lives of my clients. Shifting the way the brain interprets stress has transformed how symptoms manifest in myself and others.

Every step of my journey has prepared me to now help others overcome their own challenges. I know what it is to suffer. But

I also know what it is to experience transformation. I have a unique gift to pinpoint what next step is needed for my clients. My many years of training, education, and my own experience allow me to carry a beautiful bouquet of healing modalities and tools that I have used to heal myself and others.

What do you want to see changed in your own life? What would it be like to learn how to heal yourself? What would it be like to quiet anxiety, stop migraines, or help joint pain and fatigue? Hope is real. Healing is available. Your invitation awaits!

AZELENE WILLIAMS

I dedicate this writeup to my daughter, Sian Williams. Thank you for choosing me to be your mother. Being able to guide you and teach you things I didn't know as a teen is so rewarding and is such an honour. I absolutely love being your mum!

MUDDY TOES AND JEAN SHORTS

by *Azelene Williams*

I was born in 1973 in South Africa with a lack of oxygen. That resulted in permanent brain damage to the left-back part of my brain. I grew up with dyslexia and left school in Year 10. For many years, I had horrible memories of my school days. Teachers classified me as dumb, stupid, and a washout.

In 1988, at the age of 15, I became a victim of a terrorist bomb blast at an ice-skating rink in Pretoria, the capital of South Africa. Only a wall in the basement of a parking lot separated other young people and me from a man who wanted to cause a lot of harm to us. The man who was instructed to place a bomb in the parking lot at Sterland was ripped to pieces when the bomb exploded in his hands while approaching the entrance to where we were standing. By the time I was 16, I was a confident, strong-willed teenager who took everything I did in my life with a passion to survive.

Shortly after I left school, I moved to Pretoria to study fashion design. That same year, I met a handsome guy, and I fell head over heels in love. Unfortunately, soon after the bond between us was established, I realised that there were a lot of unexplained things happening in our relationship. Things I was not used to while growing up in a loving home. Our relationship soon escalated into physical and emotional trauma.

I was in my mid-teens and was not aware of the term "grooming." It was only years later, and after I escaped from this relationship, that I realised that the grooming phase in our relationship was stretched out over a period of a year. In the first year of our relationship, I gave consent and lost my virginity. Soon after I lost my virginity, a lot of things changed in our relationship. His kind words turned into vulgar comments. He would shout things to me like, "No man wants a second-hand girl like you!" That was the first taste of the verbal abuse I experienced. He made me feel dirty and used, and the biggest mistake I made was not to talk to anyone while I had the chance. Today I still regret that I gave consent at such a young age.

Being strong but innocent at the same time was one of the things he loved about me. The challenge for any abuser is to break their victims down. Bit by bit. For them it is all about power and control. The physical abuse started with little bumps here and little slaps there. He made me believe that I deserved everything that was happening to me. I was scared at that point, but it was hard for me to comprehend what was going on. No one had ever taught me about the different forms of abuse, or what the cycle of abuse looked like.

And the consent I gave as a teen, was never consent, it was sexual abuse because I was underaged, and he was 23. Slowly but surely, I started to lose contact with my friends and family, and not long into our second year, I found myself isolated from people who cared for me and loved me. Not long into the relationship, I started working for him and didn't have my own income and ended up being financially dependent on him. My relationship soon spiralled into a much more dangerous phase. The man I thought I loved was so out of control. One day after I got off the phone with my dad, my dad surprised me with the news that he got me an apartment. He jumped up from the couch where he was sitting and grabbed his .38 Special Revolver. As I tried to run away, he pointed it at me through an open window. He shouted Stop! And as I turned around, I looked into the barrel of his revolver. Seconds later, he pulled the trigger. The bullet that was meant to kill me that day missed my face by 10 cm, the bullet had penetrated the wall next to my head instead. It was so close to my face I felt the cement particles on my skin and in my eyes. I still wonder today if he missed me on purpose that day or if it was just not my day to die. At this point, I feared for my life, but because of his power and control over me, I went back to him for another year of physical and emotional abuse. The back cover of my book BROKEN Breaking the Silence describes the night I escaped his abuse. It took me years to walk away.

I get asked so many times, "Azelene, why did you stay?" For me, it was guilt, shame, and most of all, fear. I looked into a barrel of a revolver when I wanted to leave; I came so close to death, and I feared for my life. So, I kept quiet and stayed. Today I know it was a biggest mistake because I could have lost my life.

This brings me to my abuser's childhood. He grew up in a family where his father physically and emotionally abused his mother in front of the kids. Unfortunately, he adopted the same behaviours and acted it out in his own relationships through learned behaviour. I know for a fact that I was not his first or last victim. His mother came to see me soon after the last assault. I lifted my t-shirt to show her what her son had done to me. His mother dropped her head and said softly, "It doesn't look that bad, Azelene! Don't worry; the bruises will go away soon." She was right, the bruises did fade over the coming weeks. The blue marks turned green, the green marks turned yellow and soon after that, they were all gone, exactly like she said. However, the internal scars have been with me for over 30 years. Today I know that sexual, financial, emotional, and psychological abuse cannot be ignored when it comes to family and domestic violence.

The more I talked about my past, the more I healed my inner child, that little girl who used to run around in denim shorts with mud between her toes. The one who didn't want dyslexia, the one who didn't want to be in the wrong place at the wrong time the night that damn bomb exploded, and the one who didn't want to be a punching bag as a teen.

Being very resilient, I overcame a lot of my trauma as a child. Between the ages of 40 and 50, I completed a Diploma in Holistic Counselling and a Bachelor of Social Work. I regularly visit schools as an experience presenter and talk about respectful relationships, coercion consent and the dangers around vaping. Today I am the counsellor and social worker I needed as a teen.

WEBSITE: www.azelenewilliams.com

LINKEDIN: www.linkedin.com/in/azelene-williams-39a89669

EMAIL: azelenewilliams@gmail.com

Azelene Williams

CLARE WILLIAMSON

*Dear Benson, thank you for breaking my heart
so wide open that I changed everything*

HOW TO STEP OUT OF VICTIM CONSCIOUSNESS INTO AWAKENED WEALTH!

By Clare Williamson

"In order to grow, we have to break"

I was standing in my kitchen making a cup of coffee when my husband walked in and said, "Did you see the email from mum about the money?"

We had been gifted $25,000 from a legacy left by a family friend.

When he left the kitchen, I started to laugh uncontrollably. I was laughing with tears rolling down my face, but they weren't tears of joy or sadness. I felt unhinged!

In 2017, I had stood in a food bank, desolate, watching my two (at the time) beautiful children rip into a box of cereal with their bare hands because they were so hungry, and I had been unable to provide for them.

I hated myself that day.

It felt like I'd hit the lowest point I could go to, and I felt that after the experience of being drugged and raped at the age of 22.

I would have given anything on that day in the food bank to have had $25,000 dollars land in my lap so easily. However, it never would have happened because I was in what I now understand was a "Victim Consciousness."

And you might be too, if money isn't coming easily to you.

However much my soul called me back then to lead and create income and impact through my soul-driven business, I couldn't get it to turn a profit, and we were sinking financially.

Now I make money easily and I believe it is because I activated my "Miracle Frequency" by understanding how to step out of "Victim Consciousness" and into "Awakened Wealth."

I am finally able to answer the call of my soul to heal the world. I can give freely and support the causes I care about—specifically, the regeneration and connection of forest fragments across the world, so we stop losing endemic species to deforestation.

If your "Soul Goal" is calling you to be more than you are today—to live more, give more, and experience more ...

You may have to "break" to get there.

On November 10, 2021, on what started out as a normal day, I broke.

But through this experience I learned something that has helped me to grow; profoundly. I understood that "Victim Consciousness" goes way deeper than "Victim Mentality," where people just blame others for their misfortune.

Victim Consciousness is a "frequency" that attracts lack into your life.

Growing up, I had been conditioned to Victim Mentality by my parents, my mum especially.

She was diagnosed with bipolar disorder when I was a baby, and she really struggled with life. It wasn't until I was older that I really saw how the tragic life I always thought we'd lived really only came from her perception.

When I'd realised this, I was angry with her. It felt like if she could have just changed her perspective and seen things differently, my whole life might have been different.

This is what brought me into coaching.

As early as eight years old, I had decided I was going to heal the world, and now I think it was because I felt like I'd failed to heal my mum. No amount of positivity could ever get her to see a bright side of life.

Her perception of life marked me profoundly. Understanding the laws of consciousness and quantum physics now, I know she created every single bad experience she had in her life, but that meant I did too. And through every single one of these experiences we both placed "armour" over our authentic true selves to mask our pain and make us feel safe.

We experienced the shadow aspect of our experiences because of trauma, and we became inauthentic to our soul's truth.

And yet, I couldn't find a place of forgiveness and peace related to my mum, which was crazy considering I had been able to forgive the man who raped me.

Mum made me feel like I got everything wrong and made bad decisions as a child through her volatile reactions. She made me fear creativity. And it was the tragedy I experienced on November 10, 2021 that woke me up to how deep this wound was.

It was a normal day. No different from any other where I would get swept up into the chaos of the daily school run with the children. I was really tired. My youngest daughter had been unwell for months and had stopped sleeping. I honestly don't remember whether I let my dog into the boot (trunk) of the car, whether the kids did or whether he just jumped in while the boot was open.

Benson was our "fourth child," but had been our second baby. He was a crazy Bernese Mountain dog who came everywhere and did everything with me. He was always by my side, always.

I know he found it hard as our family grew. He didn't like all the noise and chaos, and he would take off and sit under the neighbour's house during the daytime, like a shepherd dog. I think we were his herd, and all he ever wanted to do was watch and make sure we were safe.

I don't remember seeing him in the car that day after I had dropped the kids off. I have tortured myself to try and remember why I didn't open the boot and beckon him out like I always did. The only thing I can think of is that he was sleeping because in the days running up to that day, we had worried he was unwell. He had been off his food and was out of character.

I found him dead in the car later that day. He had overheated.

And after that experience, it took everything I had, to the core of my soul, to recover from what I had done with strength and dignity.

In the days that followed, I didn't know how I was ever going to be able to get over the guilt that I was the reason he was no longer in our lives. My husband and children were heartbroken. We grieved for him like we had lost our child.

Dogs teach us about unconditional love and forgiveness and after that day, I turned inward and asked myself how I could go forward and accept this gift he had given me.

I was standing at the crossroad that my mum must have stood at a thousand times ... that we all have stood at, multiple times through our lives.

In front of a decision between healing and letting go, with love and forgiveness, or choosing to be a victim to our circumstance and living a tragic life.

There is always light in the darkness, but you have to be willing to go into the darkness to find the light. "In order to grow, we have to break." I went into the darkness in the months that followed losing Benson. I saw things that made me feel very uncomfortable. I realised how, even though I had gone from standing in that food bank to being a six-figure coach, that I was just as broke at a higher pay check because I had lost my freedom and peace of mind to a busy business that wasn't even a conscious expression of who I am and the exact thing I am here to do with my life.

I was still living unconsciously from limiting beliefs about myself and money.

After Benson, I began to live my life in ritual. Integrating and embodying my own work was the only thing that got me through those early days and the same practices I had taught my clients to heal their trauma saved me as well.

I began connecting with the energy of me, but also beyond me every single day, and I began to truly understand who I am at a soul level—enough to confidently commit to be a full and radical expression of myself.

This level of truth is the frequency of higher consciousness. This is your Miracle Frequency. The destination of the journey from Victim Consciousness to Awakened Wealth. It is the journey that Benson gifted me to love myself, forgive myself and have more compassion and empathy towards others as well.

When I had opened the car door that day and found Benson slumped over in my car seat, I had this sickening remembering of how this was just another way "I get everything wrong and make bad decisions." It brought my feeling of being fundamentally flawed and broken right up to the surface, and I suddenly realised that in my plight to heal the world, I was seeing it from the same consciousness. Other people and other things were broken because it was me who was broken. Everything is a mirror of what we believe.

I decided not to give into the reality that this limiting belief was creating anymore, and I set the intention to shift into the person I have always had the potential to be without the "armour" I wore to keep myself safe from judgement. And I committed to facing the vulnerability and discomfort of this step.

I now know that our triggers are our gifts. They wake us up when we don't know we are sleeping.

My mum has always been one of my biggest triggers. In one of the breathworks I did after losing Benson, I saw her as a little child, and I saw her for the truth of what she was ... a little girl who never felt loved enough to believe she wasn't also broken and a burden.

And she never got to heal this limiting belief.

This new perspective set me free from my own. My ego began to quieten, which enabled me to more easily make changes to feel more aligned in my life and business.

I stopped being quiet. I quit fearing being wrong, and I stopped seeing others as having more authority!

I stopped playing small.

I began to see differently and love differently. I gave myself permission to celebrate all of who I am and the fact that I can be a unique expression of gifts because of my story. It is my blueprint of how to make a difference. It is yours too.

I opened a clearer channel to Source, and I accepted that I am a Healer, a Lightworker. I am the light in other people's darkness with my story and my soul talents.

There is a powerful quote I love from Aubrey Marcus:

> *"You have to take a unique risk to write your unique story."*

I understand that deeply now and how the feeling of being willing to lose everything allows you to gain everything you want. In turn, that helps you choose the story you write that sets you free to live an aligned and beautiful life.

Before Benson, I believed that being all of who I am, creating money through my passion, expressing my creativity, joy and radical self-expression couldn't make money. Today I have completely pivoted my business and am using all my soul talents to help other visionaries create Awakened Wealth.

My playground is my business, delivering high-level programmes through a 1:1 intensive and a holistic mastermind. I've also stepped into hosting eco-conscious, transformational retreats and answered the call to study Shamanism.

The step from Victim Consciousness to Awakened Wealth will heal the world as it transcends our consciousness and takes us within to find the answers to our problems so that we become powerful creators of everything we have in our lives.

If you are ready to activate your Miracle Frequency like I have, connect with me here: https://Shor.by/cw_full_circle and click the '7x7 Method' to get access to my free app to support you!

DIANE BÉLANGER

Dedicated To my husband Marc who continues to provide immense support, love and encouragement. You are my rock!

And to my parents for the true and deep human values they instilled in me during my upbringing! You are always close to my heart!

AT THE DAWN OF A RENEWED LIFE!

by *Diane Bélanger*

A tragic family event changed what I felt was a great life, sending it into a downward spiral, but most importantly, it allowed me to discover my true passion and reinvent my life. It wasn't easy, but I took one day at a time, trusted my intuition, and listened to my true desire. Let me bring you through a journey on how to connect your body, mind, energy, and soul to understand and heal yourself in a brand new but simple, gentle, and amazing way!

In 2007, the summer was going great. I had received a promotion at work, becoming a regional director for a federal government department. My husband and I had started a new hobby, golf. However, my life was about to change. On July 23, my father died in a fire, which destroyed our family house in the middle of the night.

As the executor of his will, I was responsible for the funeral arrangements, numerous legal processes, investigations and cleaning the land of fire debris. It took me almost six weeks of daily involvement to complete all these tasks. This event and the work I had done during the six-week period sent me into a serious downward spiral.

My family doctor recommended a few weeks of rest accompanied by therapy and medication. I must point out that I refused the latter. During the first few weeks, I felt something was off. I had various health issues, which arose out of the blue like extreme fatigue, low blood pressure, uncontrollable bursts of emotion (sadness, rage, disbelief, and strong distressing memories of the fire), back pain, anxiety, panic attacks, headaches, heart palpitations and insomnia. Every night, I would wake up at 3:30 a.m., the exact time we had received the call about the fire. Around the fifth week, I started to have upsetting dreams, I felt more fatigued, I was sad, and I was reliving the traumatic event with flashbacks, and started to avoid my regular activities and stay at home. I was eventually diagnosed with depression and PTSD. Contrary to my childhood belief and upbringing, I decided to seek psychotherapy and alternative holistic medicine instead of following traditional western medicine.

Instead of using medication to put plaster on my wounds, I decided to face my wounds one by one, acknowledging them, creating a sacred space to reconnect with myself, but most importantly, changing my thoughts.

This left me with the challenge of taking charge of my own health in a new way, but most importantly, it absolutely changed my life. After four long months of intense therapy with guided imagery, core transformation, a transcultural shamanic journey, acupressure, reiki, meditation, holistic coaching and naturopathic services for my nutrition and supplements, I was getting better each day. During the first three weeks of intense therapy, I felt a major shift within. Weeks turned into months, and I was back on track, stronger than ever.

I truly believe that every thought you have and every word you say has an effect on your life, your cellular memory, and your body as a whole. The difference is whether you continue to suffer (physically and mentally), live in disbelief, stay in victim mode, worsen the situation, wear a mask or you start a new journey, a new life and open up new pathways to healing.

Throughout my healing journey, I realized that my body had given me previous signs to stop but I had not listened. I was disconnected from my feelings, my intuition and my body as a whole.

Four years after my father's tragic death, I saw death and life in a different way. I gained a totally new perspective of life. My career was no longer important. I had found a new way of being and living. I was a successful human resource executive. However, I decided that I no longer wanted to be in that stressful environment. My heart and soul were seeking something greater and more passionate.

I decided that if I could be successful at conquering all those health challenges (body, mind, soul, energy), I wanted to find a way to help others, offering a "one-stop shop" where clients would could have their challenges addressed as a whole (body, mind, soul, energy) instead of only partially. I developed a plan, started my learning journey and obtained various licenses and accreditations to start my own business. In 2011, I started my business part-time. In 2018, after much reflection, I retired from my stable government job to follow my true passion. I opened **New Era Learning and Wellness Center Inc.** full-time.

Over the last 11 years, I have helped thousands of people from all walks of life with mild to severe health, personal and emotional challenges:

- Physical health issues (back pain, extreme fatigue, heart palpitations, stomach ulcers, cancer, Parkinson's, fibromyalgia and a variety of other body pains, just to name a few)

- Mental health issues (anxiety, social phobias, dementia, insomnia, panic attacks, suicidal thoughts, PTSD, negative thoughts and uncontrollable behaviors, just to name a few).

Since 2011, I have and continue to offer consultation to my clients to understand their individual needs to achieve success in all areas of their lives by creating a tailored personal growth and healing program. I enjoy guiding people from around the world through their own journey to create the life they truly desire. I offer a variety of holistic health services and consultations, coaching, mentoring and personal growth training in a fully bilingual environment.

Through tailored individual work sessions, I guide my clients to develop their own solutions, mainly through powerful questions, but mostly by focusing on them. I guide them to tap into the power of their imagination to foster healing at all levels of their being and enhance their functioning and/or performance at all levels of their life.

I use a holistic approach which combines three interrelated aspects: mind, body and spirit.

As part of the **"Mind"** aspect, I mainly use guided imagery and core transformation, where I show my clients to tap into their unconscious mind by using a variety of tools adapted to their specific needs. These tools and techniques allow my clients to break through their internal blockages and limitations.

As part of the "**Body**" aspect, the focus is on energy medicine. I help clients understand their body pains and stresses, triggers, and energy flow as a whole. I teach and assist clients to connect to their internal bio-energy and physiology using body reflexology, meridians and chakras alignment. The techniques and processes allow the clients to connect with their intuition, feel grounded, obtain clarity of mind, attain higher vibrant energy, and empower themselves.

As part of the "**Spirit**" aspect, the focus is on the heart, soul and energy connection. Using elements of Transcultural Shamanism, my clients can now deal with the spiritual aspects of their illnesses in order to restore balance and harmony in their life.

I am now making a difference in people's life, guiding, helping, and training them in their personal healing journey to find the true meaning of self-love, reconnecting with their soul, understanding their body triggers, but mostly, creating the life they truly deserve and desire.

As a result of my personal growth and looking back over the last several years, I now understand that I had to lose my father to have access to a renewed life more fulfilling than I could have imagined it.

> *"Your vision will become clearer when you look into your heart. Who looks inside awakens."*
> – Carl Jung

Learn and become the best version of YOU! Are you ready for the next chapter of your life? Let's connect to tailor a program to learn how to become the best version of you. I offer various personal growth training, one-on-one holistic coaching and training, naturopathy services and much more.

WEBSITE: **www.dbelanger.ca**

LINKEDIN: **www.linkedin.com/in/diane-belanger-75b09981**

EMAIL: **newera@dbelanger.ca**

FACEBOOK: **New Era Nouvelle Ere**
https://www.facebook.com/diane.belanger.984

PHONE: **1 506-962-1770 (Canada)**

Diane Bélanger

REV. DR. EDIE DE VILBISS

This work is dedicated to the heroes in the headset who keep our emergency services going. Thank you.

THE SEARCH FOR MY BEST LIFE

by *Rev. Dr. Edie De Vilbiss*

"The snake is out of its cage again!"

Frantically, I dart around my house, looking in corners, behind, and under furniture. No luck.

Terror burns my veins. Pounding chest. Short breath.

"What is a snake doing in my house? I would never . . . "

Suddenly awake.

There is no snake in my house. I would never live in a house with a snake in a cage.

A bleary glance at the clock. If I get right back to sleep, I could still get a full six hours in before my kindergartner gets home from school. When the two older ones get home, we'll eat supper. With any luck I can get in a two-hour nap before work tonight.

I'll never get back to sleep with my heart racing. I can't go on like this. I have three more overnight shifts before my weekend.

Working in 911 emergency communications sometimes demands difficult things. It's just part of the job.

What is this nightmare trying to tell me? This is the third time that stupid snake has slithered out of its cage and terrified me. It is large, and colorful, and dangerous; I fear it will squeeze the life out of me and swallow me whole.

Sleep deprivation is going to kill me.

———————————

Since sleep was out of the question, I spent my days looking up options for getting help. It seemed impossible to find.

The doctor just wanted to prescribe sleeping pills.

They made it hard to wake up. The hangover from the sleep medication was worse than the grogginess of sleep deprivation. That option was out the window.

The agency had an Employee Assistance Program, and I could get an appointment with a therapist in about six weeks.

Six weeks? I'm not going to sleep for the next six weeks?!? I'll take it. I'm not sure I'll make it six more weeks at this rate, but I'll try. I thought.

I tried alcohol.

Mr. Wonderful had left me, and my paycheck was already stretched thin. Going to the bar was out of the question, I had to get the kids to school. Having a beer alone at 8 am just seemed wrong.

———————————

My friend is a wise nurse. Her wicked sense of humor and practical approach to life kept me grounded. Our schedules didn't often allow us to get together. This dinner was a rare treat.

"We had the saddest case in labor and delivery last week." She looked downcast as she said it.

"We had a baby born with signs of both sexes, poor thing. You see, this tragic child had both a penis. . . and a brain." Janie's wicked grin slid across her face.

Laughing felt so damn good. How long had it been since I felt good?

"Janie, I still have four weeks until I see a counselor. I haven't had a good night's sleep on this rotation yet. And I still have a couple of months to go. What am I going to do?"

———————————

Sleeplessness was not my only issue.

Impatient with callers, cranky on the radio, and snapping at co-workers, I was not any fun to be around at all.

My core was hollow, whatever was supposed to fill me up was gone.

My physical health declined rapidly. High blood pressure, gall stones, and general aches and pains plagued me.

My husband had left. My children walked on eggshells to spare themselves my wrath. And I didn't even have the energy to cry.

Listening to other people's tragic lives had taken its toll on mine. The pain in my heart clouded every interaction.

Compassion Fatigue happens when the cumulative trauma of the work causes a cluster of symptoms that strip away quality of life. It magnifies the worst of a person's personality and diminishes the best. The physical, relational, emotional, and spiritual effects are devastating.

Therapy slowly patched me back together. My counselor helped me decide that I would leave 9-1-1 and go to school. I didn't know how I would afford leaving a good job, much less paying for my education. And yet, I knew I couldn't not do it.

When I left 9-1-1, I thought my struggle with mental health issues was over. The treatment for Compassion Fatigue had me back to myself somewhat. At least I could sleep again. The snake no longer slithered in my dreams.

I still carried the extra weight I had put on. With full-time work and full-time school, I had no time for therapy. Plus, I no longer had the EAP. I needed to continue my journey without support.

The knowledge of the tools I needed was helpful. I knew I needed to take care of my body. I just didn't know how.

It also became apparent that caring for my personality, my way of showing up in the world, would be beneficial.

I would start a diet and exercise program, and quit just a few weeks later. My weight just went up two to five pounds a year. It's not that bad! This was the pattern I had started in 9-1-1 and it simply continued, for twenty years.

For a few years after Mr. Wonderful left, I sought to find a mate again. I found that it was impossible for me to get close to anyone. I was too cynical, demanding, and intolerant.

I decided to figure out how to love myself before trying to love anyone else.

My education to become a licensed counselor was phenomenal. The down side was trying to apply the knowledge to myself.

My academic journey led me to pay particular attention to how people change in this world. I dove deep into studying addictions and recovery.

It became clear that habits are at the root of everything in our lives. Our habits of thought and behavior are 40-70% of our days. Dial in the right habits, you'll dial in the life you want.

But how? I tried and failed to change myself so many times. I knew what to do, but not how to do it! It took some time and a lot of work to get there... but I got there.

My quest to discover a process that works has paid off. I cracked the code, so you don't have to.

In my journey, through the *Best Life Process*, I've accomplished much.

- Completed my doctoral program both using and teaching this process.
- Met and married my wonderful husband.
- Survived my grief journey when he died less than a year later.
- Have gotten an auto-immune condition into remission.
- Dropped 85 pounds from my 5'3" frame.
- Kept the 85 pounds off for the past two years.
- Shared this process with others and seen fabulous results.

Katie credits our work together with improving her relationship with her husband. Casey is helping her children with managing their emotions through sharing what she's experienced with me.

My Best Life Process is adaptable to your goals. Your best life awaits your actions. Reach out to me and let's get you on the journey to truly have a life you love. Your life is worth your effort.

Your first step in the *Best Life Process* is to access the free 911: Self Care Blueprint, here:

Contact Edie through here: https://linktr.ee/ediedevilbiss

FARITA KHAMBATTA

I dedicate my chapter to my beautiful family and to every person who has felt they weren't enough exactly as they are. You're a gift, you're amazing, you're a miracle - Farita, xo

FLIP THE SCRIPT

by *Farita Khambatta*

Here's a question for you, if you had a choice between happiness or misery, what would you choose?

In theory, I should have had a great life—a stable home and family, a good education growing up in beautiful Australia and yet something, somewhere had gone terribly wrong.

In June 2001, I began seeing blood in the toilet, and after the first of what was to be many not-so-fun colonoscopies, the results were in—I was diagnosed with an incurable autoimmune disease, Ulcerative Colitis, a form of Inflammatory Bowel Disease.

And in that moment, my life changed forever.

At my worst, I didn't want to live. My days and nights were a living hell of violently painful and bloody stools that came with such intensity and frequency that I dreaded waking up each day. My extreme blood loss also led to dangerously low iron levels, hair loss, extreme joint pain and perpetual fatigue. Mentally, I suffered from panic attacks, loneliness, and depression. Even with the support of my family, I felt utterly alone and helpless.

Ulcerative colitis sucked every single joy out of my life.

Food became my enemy. My days were filled with sadness and pain. Fun faded to a distant memory. Going to the mall, walking the dog, hanging out with friends, going out to dinner and a movie, things we all take for granted became impossible—it was all too hard, scary, and stressful. The worst was the anxiety when I sat in a car. I'd pray to God from the moment I got in until the moment I got out that I would make it without an "accident". Sometimes I was lucky, sometimes I wasn't. I would starve myself if I had to leave the house "just in case." I lived in constant fear.

In 2008, I ended up in hospital with an extreme bacterial infection in my gut and a highly inflamed colon. After two weeks, I was released, and life went on. I even began to have some semblance of a normal life until another brutal flare hit me in 2015. The colonoscopy report looked like something out of a horror movie but with the help of my specialist and stronger medications, I stabilized.

But the worst was yet to come.

Fast forward to June 2021. As I awoke from another colonoscopy, my doctor looked at me with a great sense of concern. I had now developed a stricture, a severe narrowing of my large intestine from scar tissue caused by years of repeated inflammation and healing. A blockage so severe that even a child-sized scope of mere millimeters could not safely fit through.

My specialist was stunned that I had no physical symptoms but having exhausted all available medical treatments, the only remaining option was a colectomy where my colon and entire large intestine would be permanently removed.

I felt anger, fear, shock and disbelief all at the same time.

In denial, I sought a second opinion, which was even worse than the first. Looking over my report, the doctor's "expert" opinion was that the stricture was dangerously close to a full blockage, and I also had a 70% chance of cancer growing within it. He advised an immediate colectomy where he proclaimed I would be cured forever.

WTF!?

The thought of cancer and seriously invasive surgery, losing my large intestine resulting in months with, or possibly a permanent future attached to a colostomy bag (poop bag), as well as destroying my fertility and any chance to start a family did not seem like a cure, but yet another cruel punishment to bear.

My heart sank as I felt that familiar feeling of fear build up inside me, and as I listened to my impending future suddenly, out of nowhere, came a moment of pure clarity.

I just said no. I don't accept this.

I told the doctor I wanted to explore alternatives before considering surgery. He looked at me with pity as if I was simply delaying the inevitable, but he could see I was determined and reluctantly agreed.

I now had six months to undo over 20 years of damage, and I didn't even know if internal scar tissue could be reversed, but my only choice was to make it happen and save my myself.

Over the years, I tried many strong medications, modified my diet, found good natural supplements and exercised when I could. Things would improve for a while and then seemingly out of nowhere, I would begin to decline rapidly and it was harder every time; the question was why? What was I missing? As I searched for answers, a clear picture began to emerge.

I had chosen misery.

Throughout my life, I had allowed myself to fall into the role of the victim. I never considered that to heal physically, I first had to heal emotionally and see a new way of life.

I needed to "flip the script."

You see, abuse and trauma can be experienced in many ways, for me, it was growing up allowing the barrage of harsh, hurtful, and critical words of others to define and diminish me.

As a child and teenager, I was bullied and teased incessantly for not being pretty, the colour of my skin, and that I was too strait-laced, boring and considered a total dork.

So as an adult, my tank of self-worth and confidence was completely empty. I didn't know how to have an amazing life. I gave up easily on my dreams convinced by others I would never succeed or be happy. Not surprisingly, any happiness I experienced quickly slipped through my fingers because deep down I was convinced a part of me felt I didn't deserve happiness.

Even when I tried to change or carve out my own direction, I was often told flat out that I was wrong, so I never learned to trust my choices and would always end up reluctantly conforming to the expectations and wants of others.

So, my whole life was such that I had ignored my "gut" instincts until one day, my gut finally found a way to be heard. There's a saying that the body weeps tears the eyes cannot shed. I had fed my body a toxic diet of negative self-talk for so many years that one day, the ulcerative colitis showed up in physical form to make me see my suppressed emotions and inner pain—and it had taken me until my condition was becoming life-threatening for me to see it.

Understanding is power, and now I knew what I needed to do.

I had to basically invent a whole new me with a whole new belief system. I had to let go of the old me, that person wasn't me anymore. It was time for the real me to come to life. I had to learn to listen to myself and become my own cheerleader, healing and happiness were not only achievable but my birthright.

For the next six months, I created a system to ensure my healing. I began to absorb everything I could about NLP (neuro-linguistic programming), the mind and meditation so that I could re-educate my belief systems and define a new story, telling myself exactly what I wanted and expected.

I created a new story for myself, one about an amazing, beautiful person who could accomplish anything she wanted. A story in which my opinion of myself was the only one that truly mattered and that I was happy and healthy.

I would visualize and meditate about being in perfect health with my colon pink, healthy, perfect and clear, and that my digestion worked perfectly with happy, friendly gut bacteria keeping me healthy and happy. I spoke to my colon often telling it how much I loved and appreciated it and that I wanted it to be with me forever.

I remember how I cried when I first asked my colon for forgiveness because I realized that despite the years of abuse I had inflicted upon it, miraculously, it was still hanging in there.

I prayed with gratitude and thanks and welcomed prayers from my devoted mother and family members who wanted to see me well. I fed my body nourishing food and certain supplements to give it the support it needed. I applied castor oil packs and researched products that were purported to reduce scar tissue. I made time to exercise my body daily and above all, I just continued seeing that image of myself as healthy, beautiful, and perfect.

Six months later, I arrived at the hospital for my review colonoscopy and remember the doctor asking me, "So, you've done what you've needed to do?" as if to ask, will you now accept surgery as your only option? And I told him with a smile, "Doctor, you are going to get through my colon, and I am going to be fine."

After my procedure, my doctor looked at me baffled once again—my colon was looking great, the stricture had reduced enough, there was no evidence of cancer, and there was no need for surgery.

As I heard those words, I felt pure joy. It felt so good to finally show the world that I have amazing abilities and the power to do what was considered impossible.

And while my dream to be a famous recording artist may have changed, I think my true desire to change the world for the better by helping people connect with their emotions and feel good about who they are remains. That is why today I am passionate about wellness and helping others overcome their personal challenges. We all deserve to experience our greatness, see how beautiful we are and live the fulfilling life that we deserve.

You have the power to change your story—just flip *your* script.

I invite you to contact me via my links if you would like to book a session with me or chat more about the specific methods I used to heal myself including RTT (Rapid Transformational Therapy), diet and supplement protocols and other techniques I practice to stay well and feel good.

www.linktree.com/farita

GREGORIO LEWIS

Dedicated to all the people like me who did not survive and to all the people like me who are currently fighting for their better lives.

THE BEGINNING: THE BEAUTIFUL LIFE OF A MURDER SURVIVOR

by *Gregorio Lewis*

My mother ... tried to kill me.

I often think about my eyes not opening up because of what I have been through.

I made a commitment to myself that I would never end my life by my own hands, although I think about it from time to time.

My family is Jewish. My mother is my personal Dr. Josef Mengele, who used Munchausen's Syndrome by Proxy (MSbP) on me. MSbP is where a caregiver/parent makes up fake symptoms or causes real symptoms to make a child look ill, and because of that, I should be dead.

When I was 14 years old, I was locked in a psychiatric facility. All were in agreement that I was not mentally ill except my parents. The professional consensus was that my parents, however, needed counseling and intervention.

Unfortunately, or fortunately, my parents had the money to buy doctors, and that is what they did. I was given an intentionally fraudulent diagnosis of schizophrenia at age 15. This diagnosis resulted in me taking approximately 80,000 psychotropic pills between 1988 and 2015, which is 28 years of treatment, health care, housing subsidies, food stamps and more at a cost of an estimated $3,000,000 U.S. taxpayer dollars.

In 2013, while I was employed by the Massachusetts Department of Mental Health (DMH) as a counselor, I obtained my adolescent mental health records. I was a ward of the Massachusetts DMH when I was an adolescent. When I obtained my medical records, it was the first time that I became aware that I had been a 28-year victim. The clinicians and psychiatrist's own handwriting proved that. My life was thrown away at age 14 in a system structured to save lives. Many knew, yet nobody protected me, much like what Scott Peck wrote about in the book "People of the Lie."

The first time I was sexually abused was in 1988 in a DMH facility. Being diagnosed with schizophrenia is not permission to violate my body, or anybody else's for that matter, but that's what happened. The abuse ended shortly before my 18th birthday.

I didn't have schizophrenia. What I had was abusive parents who gaslit and labeled me, even if not with conscious intent, as a mentally ill person for their benefit. My parents threatened a still active psychiatrist into egregiously changing my medical documentation from non-symptomatic to being gaslighted to having schizophrenia.

My first sexual experience was forced upon me in this psychiatrist's office by a woman in the house I was locked in while I was impotent and had grown breasts due to the effects of the psychiatric meds I was put on. The day before Thanksgiving 1988, I showed the psychiatrist that I had grown breasts. On Thanksgiving Day 1988 at my parent's home, one of my older cousins was wrestling with me, and my shirt got pulled up. I freaked out because I had breasts.

When I freaked out, the narrative that I was a mentally ill person was solidified with my whole family. Thirty-four years later, that narrative still shockingly persists, despite my extended family's extensive white collar professional background. My mother was an active member of her local Jewish community, and my father was a successful corporate lawyer.

It's been five years since I've had a family, but unfortunately, I don't know what a family is supposed to be like because of how I was treated. For 28 years I was a toilet, and so people treated me accordingly. It was normal because a toilet serves one purpose, and because I was sick, I was easily flushed. Except I never had symptoms that met the criteria of a mental illness.

I don't understand why I've chosen to live after all the abuse, as I could have ended it all even today and never again have to live with the unhealed trauma of others.

But for me, now I have a purpose to share my true-life experience so that not only can others know that they are not alone but so, as a society, we can be more aware that medical gaslighting, psychiatric neglect, and family abuse is real, and that for some of us, psychotropic medication is the primary form of abuse.

On May 1, 2015, I took my last pill acting as my own defiant superhero and as crazy as I thought the psychiatrists were, they and my other doctors at Boston Medical Center told me that if I didn't stop taking the psychiatric drugs, I would never get better. So, because of them and their willingness to defy the standard medical model with which they were indoctrinated into, I am healing with each day, and I'm healing with each new sunrise.

For 10 years, I worked as a Certified Peer Specialist. It was and still is my passion to help others transcend the very worst things that can be done to a person. Due to my compassion and intention to love myself in the way that all children and humans are worthy of, I continue in my loving act of defiance and empowerment. Like all human beings, I was born pure and it is my human right to be the truth that my story is.

While studying to become a Certified Peer Specialist, as part of my internship, I created a support group format based on my personal daily recovery journey.

Ultimately, after years of volunteering, I self-published the *Better Days: a Mental Health Recovery Workbook*, with over 10,000 copies in print.In 2015, I was an eyewitness to a mental health colleague sexually exploiting rape survivors in a psychiatric hospital. I was mandated to report the abuse, and I did.

You have understood correctly that there is something wrong in my life involving the Massachusetts Department of Mental Health. The same institution which funded my paychecks was also the same institution who was responsible for my 28 years of torture via psychiatric medication.

May 2015 was the month that I finally liberated myself from 28 years of abuse. It was obvious that I sustained psychiatric drug-induced Chronic Brain Impairment (CBI) from the medication, and I began seeking treatment with a neurologist at Boston Medical Center. Thankfully, cannabis was prescribed to me, and it helped me heal in remarkably profound ways.

I now know that I should have kept my mouth shut about the abuse that I witnessed but I loved working as a mental health provider, and I cared about those people's lives.

Two birds were killed with one stone, and I am both birds. I'm a murder survivor, and yet, my abuse story was silenced and I was erased, by the same institution, 28 years apart , for similar reasons.

Perhaps because I have been a punk rocker since I was a teenager, I somehow had it in me to stand up and fight for what I believe in because injustice is intolerable to me.

Being expendable hurt me; being erased forced me to fight. I was given two ultimatums, one by my family, and one by my colleagues. If I didn't stop talking about what happened, I would have neither a family nor a career.

So, I accepted the consequences for choosing to be free and for telling my story.

I became homeless in January 2018 and left everything that I knew behind. I jumped, as illustrated by the comedian Steve Harvey during an outtake of Family Feud, and spent more than a year traveling to most of the European countries sharing my survivor story and giving professional training for mental health workers. On some days, I would earn $900 U.S. dollars, despite being unable to get work back home.

I'm a stubborn and difficult but ultimately kind and loving man. I made the decision to stay alive and tell my story, no matter what. So, maybe I set myself up for a life of misery or perhaps a life of beauty.

I have published six books about healing from trauma, and I intend to experience my last natural breath. My heart is pure, and love flows through my veins. Love and honor are the most important things in the world to me. Maybe by sharing this story with the world, some people will care enough about me and others to somehow help make everything better because I can't do it all myself.

I know that this story will become well known to the millions who will read it. Just the process of writing this chapter and sharing this information with the public in a form that facilitates the possibility that many people may learn about it, results in my chances of living and healing more possible.

Thank you for taking the time to learn the truth about the real Gregorio "Craig" Lewis. I love you all wherever you are.

WEBSITE: **sanityisafulltimejob.org**

EMAIL: survivingtheimpossible@gmail.com

Gregorio Lewis

INNA PINKHASOVA

I dedicate this book and my work to my son Sammy. Together we had a long journey full of twists and turns and I would not have missed a moment of it. His unique personality and warm spirit are what keeps me going. He is my constant inspiration to help other children and families in need.

THE BEST LAID PLANS…

by *Inna Pinkhasova*

PLANS ARE THINGS THAT CHANGE

When we think of our life and how we want to live it, we make plans. We dream of who we will be when we grow up, and as we get older, we start to create a path to make those dreams a reality. I was on my way to those plans, but life has a funny way of letting you know that you are not really in charge.

One of my plans, was to have a family but not the way I expected. I love kids, so when I found out I was pregnant with my son, despite it not being exactly as planned, I was ecstatic. My husband (then boyfriend) and I were not yet married and our relationship was still very new, but we were both so happy about becoming parents. The idea that we were having a child strengthened our bond and, with his arrival, we became an instantaneous, happy family.

FRIDGE HORROR

About eighteen months later our happiness stopped dead in its tracks. Our beautiful baby boy was diagnosed with ASD (Autism Spectrum Disorder). Needless to say, we were shocked, and the joy we first felt as new parents quickly slipped away. Suddenly, the world and everything in it felt dark for our new little family. Our long-awaited and only child was ill – or so we thought.

Autism? What did we know about this? Frankly nothing. Neither of us knew anything about autism or why this would have happened to our child. We had no family history of it that we knew of and no idea why one child is autistic when others are not. All we knew was that our son could not talk, did not look into our eyes when we called his name or even during cuddles and endless affection. He was unable to express himself, what he wanted, or needed, what was upsetting, frustrating or even to let us in on his simplest needs like hunger or thirst. Instead, his method of communication would result in severe tantrums. This simply broke our hearts. We were paralyzed, unable to do much more than witness our baby suffer. We were at a complete loss as to what to expect, what to do, and how to even accept the news.

Unfortunately, and to my surprise, at that time, there weren't as many resources as we have now. The clinics were putting very little effort into training the families and children dealing with the effects of autism. The advocacy was limited, new parents did not receive very much guidance, and most clinics had a "no parent to therapist communication" policy. Many therapists, and even their supervisors, were not responsive, no clinical goals were appropriate and often there was no one to talk to.

EPIC REVELATION

After two months of grieving, I was at wit's end. Then one day, something new happened. I was playing with my son and I witnessed something incredible. He sat by the window in our living room and stared out the window for nearly an hour. He sat watching the cars on the busy street, people walking by, and seemed to be fixating on the tall trees around the old apartment buildings (and I stood by dumbfounded at his calm resolve). His tantrums stopped. His speech impairment, frustration, and autism-related behaviors were not happening during those long, lovely minutes. At that moment, near to tears, I saw our son again. I saw a little boy – our little boy, someone who was just like the rest of us, but with a label that read "Autism Disorder Diagnoses." This was my Aha moment, my realization that this title, this detailed report with all its assessments and conclusions, did not define my son! I watched him closely as he watched the world outside our window and realized that he was a part of it all, regardless of his apparent disconnect. This was his world, too! I stopped asking "why us" and shifted my thinking to, *how I can help him better understand and navigate the world he is looking at through that window.*

KEEP A GRIP

At the time our son was learning to deal with the world, I returned to "my plans." I went back to UCLA to study for my undergrad degree and my dream career, practicing law. After graduation, I was offered jobs with startups, corporations, and even some partnership opportunities. I received my Bachelor's Degree at a later age than some of my fellow students. Prior to returning to school, I had gained extensive experience in business operations, marketing, and sales, yet my passion remained in law.

FOLLOW YOUR HEART

I explored all of my post-graduation options but I could not bring myself to take any of them. I declined every offer that was on the table and instead, I followed my heart. It told me that what I really wanted was to choose being a mother. I chose my son's intervention, and the moment I put my career on the back burner, my life changed. I started researching his diagnosis and began compiling resources. I learned about Autism, ABA, Speech therapy, Occupational Therapy, Physical Therapy and sought out the best professionals available.

I am a strong believer that everything starts at home, so our son was receiving intensive intervention but not just from me and my husband. I learned how vital it was and is for kids who have been diagnosed as on the Autism spectrum to have a strong team that consists of school facilitators, an ABA team, and most importantly, family – the family who does not give up, a family specifically trained and knowledgeable in the intervention.

Parents' involvement is an imperative component of our children's intervention. There are questions we must know the answers to:

- What do we do at home?
- Do we use the same methodologies the clinical team is using?
- Do we know how to follow through?

- Do we understand the importance of applying reinforcement procedure?
- Do we even know what autism means?

And if we don't know the answers, who can show/train/guide us through it all?

ACCEPTANCE

By the time he turned four, we had a created strong and solid team for our son. He started to speak and express himself more. His interests and talents were more pronounced and his charm was shining through. He was able to look at us when he spoke and his motor skills were improving. I treated him no differently than any neuro-typical child; he participated in dance recitals, group piano lessons, swimming, and we even tried out some sports activities. I will admit, those days were hard for us. He was improving, but his tantrums were still uncontrollable. He still showed aggression and frustration but we did not give up. His instructors were patient and supportive. I even brought in an ABA therapist to shadow him in each class as long as he stayed in the mainstream. I tried to balance out the treatment of his disorder with a typical lifestyle of a neuro-typical child—connecting his world with ours.

By five years old, he was making even more progress, but something dawned on me that year. I asked myself, *Am I trying to change him, to make him into someone he is not? Am I still not fully accepting that this disorder has befallen my child?*

No, I thought. *I am not trying to change him. I am trying to help him and provide the absolute most support possible.* Both my husband and I made sacrifices; we spent years on his intervention simply because he is our son, our child, our baby.

WHY I CREATED THE ENRICHMENT INTERVENTION FAMILY CENTER (EIFC)

Momtrepreneur

The more I learned, the more I realized that this was about more than my son. This was my real life's calling. I realized that my real passion is life was to help other families like ours. I saw that so many families were lost, dazed and confused when they got the diagnosis and were floundering, seeking real help. I made it my mission to see to it that other parents would not feel like as if they are alone in this journey. I made it my goal to provide maximum support for as many children diagnosed with ASD and the families that loved them. That is my WHY and so, I decided to open up a family center for these children and their families.

Ego vs. Heart

Opening up a business is equivalent to birthing a baby. This particular baby was unplanned. First and foremost, I had to ask myself how much I wanted it. Was this coming from my ego or from my heart? After a lot of soul searching, I believed that my desire and passion to help others who were going through what my family was experiencing overpowered all my fears and doubts and validated my true intention. So, I forged forward and opened the center.

Safe Harbors

The EIF Center provides services for families who have children diagnosed with autism disorder. I have the word "Family" in our title because we not only help kids, we also help their caregivers. Often, we don't realize how much stress is on these caregivers. We can't take expect that they are "just fine" and that all the focus must be on the child. Family members need guidance, support, and training too, sometimes even more so.

To that end, we facilitate clinical meetings on a weekly basis with our parent and guardian workshops. We carefully design treatment plans for each family and our clinicians review those treatment plans with all the caretakers in the child's life to ensure quality, as well as monitor progress. It is my job to oversee the quality of each department, take measures as needed, and administer and execute new strategies. It's exciting and rewarding. When I'm out in the field, I am known for meeting with families, connecting with each family member, and learning more about their culture and home environment. I learn so much from each child and his or her family and my staff and I take pride in serving our clients with a more personal approach. We run our clinical programs efficiently and effectively but we never forget that we are dealing with people, people who are often scared, confused, and even a little lost as to how to navigate these difficult waters. We love being able to steer them to safe harbors as often and as much as possible.

Unwavering Commitment

I am most proud of how our kids have grown, how our parents are now more trained and less afraid to apply the knowledge they've gained. I am proud to learn that parents are no longer afraid to come out to the communities with their children because they have the resources and support they need. I am proud of our incredible team and the strength of our clinical department, the challenges we faced, and how far we have come. All the growing pains we experienced in our first few years did not put us out of business or break us apart!

It has taken and still takes a lot of hard work. But I am blessed with an incredible family and a place I can call home. I am blessed that I have come across people in my life who share the same vision that I do and see beyond the diagnosis of the medical condition that is ASD. It is that shared vision and connections and the belief that we can do better to support our children, the parents and caregivers, and the community that led to forming EIFC.

This requires intention, vision, and unwavering commitment. My team and I committed to doing our very best with everything we know, everything we have, while staying open to new possibilities.

The Strength Within

The most vital part of it all on this journey has been believing in myself. At first, I pointed fingers at anything I had gone through in life that "caused" a delay in making my dreams come true. I used those things as an excuse for why I wasn't getting what I wanted. Overcoming the barriers of personal fears and doubts has helped me attract the strong, ambitious, and loyal people that are in my life today.

The Point of a Breaking Point

I tell our ABA parents—during intervention...

"You will be met with the impossible. You will hit what will feel like plateaus and dead ends. That is when you will let the diagnoses carry more weight and more power than it deserves. It's when giving up will seem so tempting. Don't give up! This is when your resilience will get you through. This is when, even though you're exhausted and feeling hopeless, you must know that you are supported and that while it may get worse before it gets better. Always keep going. Your children are worth it. You are helping to expand their world so they may claim their rightful space in it. Your perseverance is the gateway to their world. Keep going!"

You've only Got Two Options

I use this philosophy in business, in relationships, friendships – or even when I go to the gym. The most vital part of success is that moment when it gets hard. There are only two options: to turn back or keep going. If I choose the latter, winning is inevitable.

There is no luck. You keep going. You gain momentum. You move forward.

And in that way, you win!

If you would like to reach out to me to discuss how I might help you or someone you know who is dealing with autism, contact me at:

To learn more about my EIF Center, go https://eifcenter.com

JULIE PAULSTON

Dedicated to my friends Dawn, RicShon, Tara and those that have walked through the fire with me and continue to believe in me, even when I lose the belief in myself. To my kids, grandkids and family, I love you more +1.

THE RISE OF THE PHOENIX

by *Julie Paulston*

> *The flames are not designed to burn us, only to burn away what no longer serves us. This is where the rise of the phoenix begins.*

Why are we so scared to rise from our own ashes? To embrace our Divine inner phoenix? To step out of the shadows of the deep recesses of our minds? Why are the ashes like a worn blanket that gives us the impression of safety and security? What is the fear that keeps us doing the same thing/s repeatedly expecting different results? Some say it is insanity, if it is, then I should have been locked up years ago with no hope of escape.

I have clung to the comfort of the ashes for so much of my life. Always making sure that "others" liked me. Doing whatever I could to fit in. Being everything to everybody and leaving nothing for myself. Wondering time and time again what was wrong with me.

We eventually get to the stage in life where The Universe starts sending signs to us to tell us that it is time. Time to rise and to shed the illusion of who the world told us who we should be. The curious paradox is this. If we don't listen to the small voice or pay attention to the small signs, the calls and voices get louder and louder. The road for our future becomes marred with potholes and debris. Yet we still press on and don't stop to realize that the overwhelm is a sign as well. We hear the calls of our inner Divinity and yet we still send them to our Spiritual voicemail. Saying to ourselves, "I will check it someday"

The signs for me became so loud and my world came crashing down within 90 days in 2020.

July 11th, I broke my wrist in 3 places.

August 27th, I got fired from the company that I had given almost 9 years of my life to and thought would be my forever place.

September 15th Hurricane Sally brought almost 3 feet of water to the interior of my home, and I lost everything I owned.

I was broken physically, mentally, emotionally and spiritually. I was "homeless", jobless and at a crossroads of my life. I fell deep into the pit of despair and at one point and time sat in the wreckage of my home and screamed at a God that I had abandoned years ago. I screamed and cried and asked why? I had followed all the gurus and did what they said to do. How could have this happened to me? I had such a good job; I had a successful life. I had amazing belongings and now I had nothing. I sat in bewilderment and confusion. Lost and alone. What I didn't realize was I had done all the "right" things to manifest the life I had. Everything that was happening was a direct result of what I believed.

The funny thing about The Universe/God/Source, whatever you choose to call it, gives us what we believe, not what we say. I had said all the right words, done all the right things. I had said the affirmations, burned the sage, collected the crystals, journaled till my hand ached. All the while knowing that I was denying my destiny. The ironic thing was that I didn't believe I was worthy deep down inside where only The Universe hears and sees. I could hear the calls from The Universe and still didn't think I was worthy of answering.

Deep inside I knew that there was more for my life, but my fear was bigger than my faith. The fear of "what would they think about me or say about me". The fear of how they would judge me for my mistakes and discover that inside I felt like a fraud and a complete failure.

This was the depth of the ashes in this journey. I had been here before multiple times, but this was new. The preconceived warmth of that blanket, keeping me stagnant and afraid until this time a light shone brighter than the depths of my despair. A light that started dim and grew brighter and brighter. It became so bright that I had no choice but to acknowledge its existence.

The Universe had my full and undivided attention. For probably the first time in my life I knew it was different. In those moments I decided to trust and have faith in the path unfolding in front of me. I stepped into my healing journey and haven't looked back.

Has it been easy? Absolutely not. Has it been worth it? Without a doubt in my mind.

Darkness can only survive when we hide our light. When we shine a light on our shadow it becomes less scary and can become one of our greatest strengths.

From the ashes I became the phoenix of my own life. I rediscovered who I was before the world told me who I should have been. I became free. I found my voice and my path has been unfolding every single day in a new and expansive, exciting way.

I started sharing my journey. Every part of it. Even the scary, icky, divisive, and controversial parts. I started living my truth in any way possible. In sharing my journey, I have been able to inspire others to do the same.

We are all here for a purpose. The challenge is that we have so much generational trauma and unhealed parts of ourselves that bind us to who society says we "should" be. When we take off the societal blinders and allow our hearts to be open, we discover the intricate, beautiful person we have always been.

Starting to heal those parts of ourselves begins our journey home. Home to who we are, who we have always been at our core. It gives us the strength to stand up to the injustices of our lives and the courage to leave that which no longer serves us.

People ask me all the time what advice I would give. I can sum it up as this.

Find the people and the things that set your soul on fire. Follow it and allow yourself the freedom to rise from the ashes of your own life and discover your own Divine inner phoenix.

Take the risk. Heal the trauma. Live your life. Discover the parts of you that you have hidden for so long. Your soul is calling to you. Please don't put it into your Spiritual voicemail. Answer the call, no matter how scary it seems.

Above all else, remember **YOU ARE ENOUGH.** You have always been enough. You will always **BE** enough. Just as you are. You are magic, stardust and Divinity wrapped into a human experience and if you could only see the Divine light that shines out from your eyes, you would never doubt your greatness again.

Connect with me...

https://linktr.ee/divinephoenixrising

JUSTINE MARTIN

To my children Zak and Ally who are the biggest supporters in all that I do.

I CHOOSE TO BE POSITIVE

by *Justine Martin*

WHAT IS A VICTIM?[1]

- a person harmed, injured, or killed as a result of a crime, accident, or other event or action
- a person who is tricked or duped.
- a person who has come to feel helpless and passive in the face of misfortune or ill-treatment.

When starting to write this chapter, I spoke to a girlfriend about me being a victim as I don't see myself as one. She was shocked and said to me that of course I was! She then proceeded to name a few things that explained why she saw me as a victim.

I have never sat for a period of time in the mindset of a victim. It's not something I've ever done.

I've never let it define solely who I am. Here is a list of some of the things that I have been a victim of in my life; there are more but these have had the biggest impact on my life.

---

1   *https://www.merriam-webster.com/dictionary/victim*

- Sexual abuse as a child
- Bullying
- Narcissistic mother
- Narcissistic partner
- Rape
- Trauma
- Domestic violence
- Fraud
- Car accidents
- Medical malpractice
- Abandonment
- Gaslighting
- Incurable diseases (Multiple Sclerosis, Melanoma, Lymphoma and Leukemia)
- Finding my partner dead on the floor

After writing this list, I sit in disbelief at everything that I have encountered, some of it is now a distant blur, and some experiences are still very fresh. I have been a victim not just once but several times throughout my 51 years. Each event has shaped the person I am today, but not having the victim mentally often goes with it.

I have continued to gain resilience from each instance, which does make it easier to cope. I'm not superhuman. I am just me. I am a positive person. I choose to live in the current moment, to learn from the past but to not remain living in the past. That would then give control to my abusers, and I will not give them or it any more power! It comes back to choice. I have chosen to build a better life for myself and my family.

Unfortunately, bad shit happens to good people, and for some of us, it keeps happening to us. But it's how we choose to handle things that determines whether we see ourselves as a victim or just someone that has had something bad happen to.

How do *you* handle bad things that other people have caused in your life?

I have been mentally damaged and physically hurt, and I would never treat anyone the way I have been to cause such pain. I've been told in the past that I forgive too easily. Maybe I do, but I don't see it that way.

I have learned to forgive the perpetrators for my own peace of mind. That doesn't mean I have forgotten what has happened to me, but for me to live at peace, to move on, have a peaceful future and be in a positive mind frame, I had to let go of the anger associated with each "victim event." I had to be kind to me and to learn to love me first.

Counselling helped me heal what others have done to me, to help me make stronger and wiser decisions in life so I don't keep making the same mistakes over and over ever again and to not become a victim again. To break the patterns that put me into situations of harm.

I was brought up with not learning boundaries and unfortunately, I took that into adulthood. I gave my children boundaries but not myself. By not protecting my inner child, it enabled me to be in situations of harm I should never have put myself in.

Don't get me wrong, those that have hurt me should never have done that, but I recognize my part in it. For example, I have repeatedly chosen narcissistic men as partners, the love bombing in the early stages of the relationship always feels amazing because that's what they want you to feel. To get you. To suck you in. But then it starts to change. Step by step. Day by day, they gaslight you, are nasty to you and make you cut off ties with your friends and family without you realizing that's what's happening.

Before you realize what is happening, you start to think you are losing your mind, but you continue to hang in there because they say they love you and that you are lucky to have them in your life! What a crock of shit!

I've been in several relationships like this, and a couple have involved domestic violence including having broken bones. Did I deserve what was done to me? Hell no! Was I a victim? Yes, unfortunately I was.

Looking back, what would I have done differently? I would have acted right away when the red flags appeared early in the relationship. I would have protected my inner child with the boundaries I now have for myself and walked away.

WHAT IS VICTORY?

- the overcoming of an enemy or antagonist.
- achievement of mastery or success in a struggle or endeavour against odds or difficulties

Having boundaries and forgiveness has enabled me to push forward and have victory in all that I am creating in my life by not letting them define what they did to me and stay a victim.

I have gone on to achieve many victories in my life pushing through the adversities I have experienced and continue to face and have gained greater resilience along the way. I am known as the Queen of Resilience. Every time life throws adversity my way, I get back up and try harder to achieve more positive things in my life and learn new things and improve myself.

In the past 11 years, I have been diagnosed with Multiple Sclerosis and was told I'd never be able to work again by a medical practitioner. I have had three heart surgeries, two blood conditions and three primary cancers all at once. I have caught partners having affairs, had my arm broken by a partner, and found my last partner dead on the floor.

People ask me all the time how I can remain so positive and achieve so much despite my disabilities and all that I have gone through. My answer is always the same. I am what I teach. I am resilient, and I choose to be positive; I choose to keep moving forward, and I choose to not see myself as a victim.

In the past 11 years, I have learned how to paint, started my first business JUZT art, became an award-winning artist, taught art wellness classes to other disabled people, and have two galleries in Drysdale and Marshall. I have represented Australia as a master's Olympic weightlifter and strongman and have won numerous medals.

I started my second business, Resilience Mindset, which comprises consulting/coaching individuals and the corporate world to overcome adversities and gain more resilience. I am a sought-after keynote speaker, telling my story as I believe it is someone else's survival guide. I have developed workshops and written books on resilience and my story.

I have also become a best-selling author, a children's book illustrator, and own four other businesses (Van-go Decals, TeamFingerprint, Morpheus Publishing, and Geelong ResidentialCleaners) all under the umbrella of Justine Martin Corporation.

I have gone on to win several business awards in the past few years.

Don't ever tell me I can't because I will always show you I can!

**https://www.merriam-webster.com/dictionary/victory

Justine Martin

KIM WARD

This chapter is dedicated to my dad, Tom. I never properly thanked you for saving my life. Thank you doesn't cover it.

LEARNING TO LOVE THE WOUNDS

by *Kim Ward*

My plan was solid. I would go to dinner with my friends, come home, and die peacefully in my bed.

My friends arrived at my house right on time. I said goodbye to my dad a little differently than usual that night as I truly thought it would be the last time that I would ever see him. I walked out of the house, shutting the door behind me, and climbed into the back seat of my friend Amy's car.

During the 20-minute drive to the restaurant, I heard the conversation between Amy and Meghan as if it were background noise. They were up front enjoying life as typical high school Sophomores and I was busy mentally playing out the rest of my night so that things would fall into place as planned.

They didn't.

We arrived at the restaurant and were seated immediately. By the time the waitress came to our table to take our order, I knew that I was in big trouble. I quickly blurted out, "chicken fingers and French fries," and asked Meghan to walk me to the restroom.

She and Amy thought I was crazy. What 16-year-old girl needed assistance walking to the restroom? What they didn't know was that I had swallowed three full bottles of pills just an hour earlier.

My speech was slurred, I couldn't stand up straight, and my vision was blurred. Instead of my friends asking me what was going on, they were extremely annoyed at the inconvenience that I had quickly become. Amy asked me to wait in her car while they ate.

I don't remember how I got to the car but I do remember exactly what happened next. Amy and Meghan were enjoying their dinner and I was looking down at my body, slouched over in the front passenger seat. It was as if I was floating in the night sky, just watching my body through the moonroof. My body started to fight back and whatever it was that was floating in the air flung itself back into my body and, as it did, rapid and projectile vomit flooded the front of Amy's car.

The girls made their way to the car, and when the passenger door was opened, I heard Amy screaming "What did you do to my car?"!

I don't believe in coincidence, especially with what happened next.

The parking lot for the restaurant was shared with a fast-food restaurant, and in that exact moment, we saw a car full of boys that we knew from school. Amy flagged them over and asked them to drive me home so that she could go to the car wash.

They transported me from Amy's car to Billy's and we started our drive home. Thank God they knew the general direction of where I lived. The boys thought my situation was hilarious. With absolutely no control of my body, Billy would quickly slam on the brakes so that my face would slam into the back of the passenger seat. They laughed wildly and continued to do that the whole way home.

No one knew exactly where my house was and I had now lost the ability to speak. As they drove around my neighborhood, someone in the car noticed my brother. They told my brother that I was in the car and needed to get home. My brother pedaled as fast as he could and the car followed.

When they pulled into my driveway, my dad was already waiting for me and I was transferred to yet another car. This time dad drove me straight to the ER.

That was a long night for all of us. I can only remember glimpses but I'll never forget the charcoal, the tubes down my nose, and the Division of Child Services sitting at the foot of my bed the next morning when I woke up.

It was a long road to recovery for me and my family, but we did recover, until we broke for good.

I may have started the inner work on myself, but my sister was slowly dying inside. We didn't know. How could we? She was a happy, successful, military police officer with her whole life ahead of her. On January 25, 2008 my only sister took her own life.

Seven years later, my mother also took her own life three days after Christmas. I was eight months pregnant with my daughter and felt like my life was worse than a Lifetime movie.

It was extremely challenging to not hate life and fall into the pit of self-destruction, but I was a wife and a mother and had to continue on with strength and courage.

I haven't quite come across a story like mine, and for a long time, I kept it close to my heart because I was ashamed, but that is just fueling the stigma.

Four years after mom died, I became as a contestant on a reality show for entrepreneurs. It was a fierce competition between entrepreneurs from all over the world. I found myself in the finals and wound up finishing the competition in third place. I was angry. I had something to prove to myself and, if I'm being honest, to the world as well.

Driving home from that competition was a pivotal phase in my life. The tears flowed, the cuss words echoed through my car, and I licked my wounds. That's when it hit me.

We learn in reflection, not in the moment.

That was my big takeaway and why I was there. I could not allow myself to play this victim role anymore. My story is too powerful not to be told for it can and will provide hope and healing.

Without a clue of what I was doing, it was placed on my heart to open a nonprofit organization for mental health awareness and suicide prevention. They say it's not what you know, it's who you know, and due to the new friends that I had made on the reality show, I was connected to the people who were able to help me get my nonprofit off the ground.

We did it! Katie's Mission is currently three years old and we are proud to offer wrap-around services including life coaching scholarships to those in need and funeral assistance when a suicide loss occurs.

Can we have a mission without pain?

I'm not 100% sure, but what I do know is that I made a decision to show up in a big way for people because of what I've been through. If I hadn't experienced all of the loss and the lows, I don't think I would be helping people the way that I do.

My mother and sister are missed every minute of every day, but through my healing and being able to help others heal, I've learned how to love my wounds; they've made me a better person.

Learn more at **http://KatiesMission.org**

Your friend,
Kim

http://www.successwithkimward.com
kim@lifebydesignsolutions.com

LISA BARRETT-OLIVER

Dedicated to my children, Curran, Cameron, McKailyn, and Delaeni who love me (and tolerate me) through the trials and the victories of our lives. And to McKenna, who was my greatest teacher and continues to look over all of us.

FOCUSED ON FAITH

by *Lisa Barrett-Oliver*

There are not many events in life that are as exciting as discovering the sex of your baby. The moment I was pregnant, my mind began wondering about who this little person would become. As this was my third pregnancy, I was hoping for a girl to round out our family of two boys. As the wand swiped over my pregnant belly, I got the news! Girl!

The next moment would define this pregnancy and my faith. The look on the technologist's face pressed fear into my heart. A moment earlier, I was smiling and excited. The very next crashed through my chest and my life.

Have you ever had an experience where you were so excited and joyful but then had it yanked away through no fault of your own. Bad luck. A statistic. The label didn't matter but the devastation did.

My daughter would only have a 40% chance of surviving birth and a 50% chance of living a normal life. That moment felt devastating and surreal but it was nothing compared to what was to come.

McKenna Faith was named intentionally. Faith would be the initial thing that would get me through this pregnancy and beyond. I knew instinctively to focus on the future. McKenna was born after a flight for life to the only hospital that was prepared for her condition. She entered this world crying and was beautiful. Nine days later, she would leave this world in silence as I wept.

When a child enters this world, they bring hope. When they leave, their hope leaves with them.

Mother and child are always connected, so as I held McKenna the day she died, I felt her die. I knew she had died before the doctors saw the flat lines of the monitors. In that moment, I felt darkness. Empty. In the many painfully long days that followed, all I wanted was the peace of death myself. To close my eyes and drift into nothing because nothing was better than pain. There are certain pains for which no cure exists, and I was confident the pain of McKenna's death could never be relieved.

Have you ever felt a sense of hopelessness? Moments when you question the value of even living? In those dark times and lonely times, there seems to be no answer. As humans, we all experience suffering. My suffering looks different from yours but the pain is similar even if it varies in degree.

The truth about life is that we all suffer. The depth and impact of that suffering varies but we all experience it. In the suffering lies a choice. We can either live in the darkness and be enveloped by it and have that darkness be the cloak that we wear every day. The scarlet letter of our existence so to speak. Or, we can choose to find a way to make our experience matter.

In the beginning, faith is what helped me see beyond suffering. Faith is a "firm belief in something for which there is no proof." I had no proof that my pain, sadness, depression would fade or leave. I had no proof that my life could be happy again. But despite the evidence, I leaned into the faith that my suffering would lift, and my life would be joyful once again. Faith, however, was up to me. The choice was up to me.

In the beginning, all I could manage was going through the day-to-day motions. I had two sons who still needed their mother. I can't imagine the extent of their sadness and confusion. They had lost a sister who was never able to even come home or be a part of our family. And now they risked losing the mother they knew before McKenna died.

I did what I could to be there for them. I vividly remember telling a friend that Curran and Cameron were the only thing keeping me alive. Even in the deepest, most intense grief I've ever experienced, there was a choice. They were my choice.

Day by day, I moved forward. I wish I could say I was an amazing example for my sons. The truth is, I struggled to be courageous. I struggled to ignore the anger and envy that rose inside me when my sister-in-law proudly announced she was expecting twins. I struggled to feel compassion or even a simple interest in other people's "trivial" problems. Unless you felt my pain, I had no interest in your pain.

In that struggle though, I thankfully had enough awareness to realize that those feelings weren't serving me or my sons. I realized that I needed to look to the future. Each day, little by little, I made the choice to focus on what I wanted in my life and that was to not focus on grief and suffering.

There's no magic formula to moving past grief. But I do know that it's something that never leaves you completely. You learn to live with it. You can't ignore it nor should you. You can honor it and heal without denying the experience.

All the shit that happens in life doesn't define us but it can refine us. We have the choice how we show up. And I believe we have a responsibility that comes with how we show up. Who we are to ourselves and to the outside world matters. As a mentor of mine said, "Memories without the emotional charge is wisdom." I don't ignore the pain but I don't cling to it either.

I started training my thoughts to go to the future, having something to create and focus on in the future is healing. I stopped wallowing in the sorrows of my grief and instead honored it and healed from it. Today, I live my life with purpose and with a focus on the future.

My children are grown. McKenna has grown in my heart and my mind as well. She will always be a part of my life, and she's a presence in my children, Curran, Cameron, McKailyn, and Delaeni, who make our family complete. Life has a way of continuing to grow us and to challenge us. As it should be.

When McKenna died, I felt like a victim of life. It wasn't my fault. It wasn't her fault. It certainly wasn't fair. There was no rationalizing it. There was no justifying it. All my emotions were driving me into a life of sorrow, a life where I lacked control and was simply a victim.

But being a victim is no way to go through life. Time, persistence and a positive future focus are the keys to becoming a victor. I have an amazing family, financial abundance and most importantly, a mindset of courage, fortitude and love.

Challenges, hard times, and difficult events are where the growth occurs. In those moments, I hold strong to the positive images in my mind of my future. Images in my mind determine my future. I do my best to focus on what I'm creating and how I positively impact others.

I continue to work within a community of future-focused people. In my business, I coach and train people to focus on the future they are creating. I encourage them to create a life of joy, financial security, courage and confidence through building a business that provides their own unique focus on the future.

The world is happy to empathize with you and validate you as a victim. But truth be told, the world doesn't need another victim. What the world needs is courage and more victors. Join me to bring more hope, courage and boldness to the world.

msha.ke/thelisaoliver

FACEBOOK: **https://www.facebook.com/lisa.barrettoliver**

INSTAGRAM: **https://www.instagram.com/thelisaoliver/**

M. SUSAN PATTERSON

Dedicated to my amazing, fierce, beautiful daughters.

LIFE UNEXPECTED

by *M. Susan Patterson*

D o they all go to the same school to learn how to escape consequences? I'm talking about manipulators and predators. I have a knack for not acknowledging the red flags in front of me and for making appalling choices in partners.

It was the 70s. I saw my future as growing my own food, using sustainable (it was called "natural" then) practices, and living a life that included helping others. I was naïve enough to believe the words spoken by the man I was dating rather than consider his actions. He led me to think we wanted the same things, while in truth, he never heard a word I said.

Eventually I realized that my goals were incompatible with his so I abandoned mine. That's what you did in the 70s. Women's Lib was in full swing, but in "Christian" circles that was frowned upon. However, secretly, Gloria Steinem was my hero.

My husband wanted an empire. A mega church, a school and university, something huge and successful. To fulfill expectations, to be a "good" wife, I read every book, attended workshops and seminars, and prayed that God would empower me to be the perfect pastor's wife, mother, partner, and church-community builder.

That was rudely interrupted on a bright, sunny, summer day, when I was informed that my husband had been in a relationship with an underage member of our previous congregation. I defended him without reservation; I knew he wouldn't put our work in jeopardy. But then he told me it was true, and, worse than that, he told me we would never speak of it again. I was forbidden to express my anger. I was told to move forward as if nothing had happened. Church doctrine taught me to obey.

So, I spent a lot of time praying. I tried to forgive him, and at the same time, I needed desperately to talk about it, to process what happened, to deal with my emotions. I begged him to let me see a therapist, a counselor, someone, anyone. He became ugly, verbally and emotionally abusive. I was struggling to hang on to my equilibrium.

Then I learned that there was more to the story. In order to avoid a certain church scandal and the possibility of being charged with a crime, he had gone first to his inner circle of pastor cronies. He did not tell me, his wife; he went to them. They arranged for him to be the pastor of a church in a different state, two thousand miles away from his problems, and two thousand miles away from my entire support system. Turns out that God didn't send us to where we were, deceit did.

Every Wednesday, and twice on Sunday, I sat dutifully in the pew and pretended to be the perfect pastor's wife. I listened to his sermons on being a good Christian, on living a truthful life, on being a good person. I stopped praying.

Ultimately, I couldn't forgive the lie that we were living in church and at home. So, I left. And everyone, literally everyone, blamed me. Until his newest conquest moved into the parsonage. The church had had enough. They asked him to leave.

I remained confused, wondering what just happened. With no support system, no money for counseling, and completely without purpose.

It is interesting how predators are expert in finding women that are naïve, vulnerable, alone. A deacon approached me with what I perceived as sympathy and compassion; naturally, I fell for it. I believed him, and we began to build a life together. It was a wonderful life for a while, in the country with gardens, wildlife, pets, and kids. Time passed, I felt something sinister creeping into our life. Something was definitely wrong, but I couldn't figure out what.

And then, on a beautiful, clear winter day, I did. He was molesting the children, mine, his, God knows who else's. The children and I went to the police, suffered through the legalities, and he was indicted by the Grand Jury. In the meantime, he left the state.

The next few years were one long foggy darkness. There were counselors, groups, anger, frustration, days and nights that blurred together. Money was always a problem, trying to have enough for counselors and food was sometimes impossible. I went to work but wasn't really there. Nothing relieved the fear and uncertainty. The children seemed to heal better and more quickly than I did, though those experiences and pain are never completely gone. You learn to just get on with life and hope it'll get better.

Time passed, and after my daughters graduated and began their own paths in life, I went back to school, finished my degree, and became a high school teacher. That was when I discovered I had a deeper and more profound compassion than I had before those unwanted, painful experiences. I connected with people, especially with my "difficult" students who were mostly inner-city kids in a racially divided town. I found my next purpose in life. I taught the "throw away" kids, written off by others. For the next nearly 20 years, I worked in that school. Most of my students became immensely successful as human beings and in careers. I still hear from many of them, letting me know they're doing well.

As it often happens, illness followed the terrible times. I was sick for eight years with one incorrect diagnosis after another. I couldn't think because of the brain fog (yes, it's a real thing), I couldn't walk or climb stairs because when I did, I couldn't breathe. There were dozens of symptoms and the doctor decided I had depression. Then I experienced a thyroid storm and came very close to death. A different doctor diagnosed me correctly, finally, and my body responded to the medicines.

During that time, I began to think about God again. He was there, waiting for the anger to subside. I began praying again and seeking a spiritual kind of growth. It took a while, but I did forgive those who had scarred me and mine. Some days I had to ask God for help to forgive. In time, I realized I was free, free from the anger and frustration, free from hate, free from the pain that held me back. That realization profoundly changed me.

Meanwhile, the medicines that saved me were drastic and difficult to tolerate. Thankfully, my daughter introduced me to essential oils which were (and are) much gentler, easier to tolerate, and allowed me to achieve health and a vibrant life. Eventually I was able to use only natural solutions for my health, and my life changed even more. My perspective changed. I added additional essential oils and herbs to address the anger I still held on to. I changed, I began to speak up, and I found my voice. As I began to share what essential oils had done for me, money fears began to melt away. Laughter and joy replaced the angry darkness. Opportunities appeared; doors opened. Using and sharing what changed me filled me with purpose and confidence. I realized I was living a completely unexpected life, different from what I planned, something much better and fuller.

I have learned many lessons, and I am a different person with a voice that is strong and resilient. I understand what victim to victory to visionary means. I have embraced the brokenness and allowed it to lead me to better things. My life is not what I planned it to be, it is so much more. What a wonderful surprise.

Links:

WEBSITE: **https://beyondwhatwas.godaddysites.com http://edgelifevision.godaddysites.com/**

FACEBOOK: **https://www.facebook.com/sudiebleu/; https://www.facebook.com/profile. php?id=100075789459781 Pieces by M.S. Munro Page**

INSTAGRAM: **https://www.instagram.com/margaretsusanpatterson/**

LINKEDIN: **https://www.linkedin.com/in/m-susan-patterson-69a507185/**

Read my book - *Pieces: A Mother's Journey: The Painful Truth of Sexual Abuse* **https://www.amazon.com/Pieces-Mothers-Journey-Painful-Sexual/dp/1736793292/ref=tmm_pap_swatch_0?_encoding=UTF8&qid=&sr=**

NEFERTITI SAN MIGUEL

I dedicate this chapter to the past, present, and future version of me.

Dear Queen Nefertiti, never lose sight of what's really important in your life, you are a walking miracle, gifted by the Gods with many talents. Some of them haven't been explored yet... you are favored by the Creative Force of the Universe. The Quantum Field plots positively in your behalf and Divine Intervention is cheering from up above the building of a happy and blooming Empire! Carry on with mighty grace, the power of nature is all around you fully resourcing all your enterprises.

Lovingly,

All the versions of Our-Royal-Selves

FROM DISTURBED SOUL TO FINDING MY HOLY GRAIL

by *Nefertiti San Miguel*

I share my transition from being a disturbed soul experiencing the depths of depression caused by **"Environmental and Mental Chaos"**, to finding inner peace and claiming my space as an international mixed media artist. I found comfort and encouragement in regularly practicing Ikebana (the Japanese soothing art of floral design), creatively intertwined it with neuroscience, and started designing a Zen environment that amplifies mental health resilience. Now, I use this transformation to inspire others to find their own Holy Grail.

My life is becoming a Masterpiece! I am so over the Moon thrilled into the next Galaxy for my ever-growing list of accomplishments! I unapologetically rock my eclectic personality wrapped in Gothic fashion to a point that many (especially the male population) might find intimidating. And before you, my dear reader, make quick assumptions about my lack of humbleness and label me as borderline arrogant, it's my mission to share with you how I got here, because this is a true story of miracles, endurance, and perseverance that might help you find your own Holy Grail!

Up until very recent years, I was constantly consumed by "**Environmental and Mental Chaos**." I allowed people dear to my heart to inundate me with more of it because they brought their own, in very generous proportions, that I absorbed because of my desire to be loved and welcomed, not barely tolerated. I constantly sacrificed my inner peace with the fool hope that eventually it would come to an end. I believed if I proved myself endlessly, I would no longer be treated as a convenience and/ or on demand. The compounding effects of that combination were quite devastating and almost lethal. I experienced chronic depression that took over my entire life, spreading like a cancer, without even being aware of it. Nobody seems to talk about such things. So, here I am, going public with my own behind-the-scenes and personal experiences to show "**family is not an unimpeachable Holy Institution**" even if its members wave the banner of living by the Gospel in strong faith. In this case, my elders were regulars at the Catholic Church and my mother was the Ambassador of Buddhist practice. What a theater that was! But people seem to be biased with the religious freaks and I was always placed in the category of being "**questionable**," hence, my pain and distress were never taken seriously.

From a very young age, I went from one misfortunate event to the next, never fully processing the root of my troubles nor inventorying in proper detail the aftermath and true damaging consequences to my well-being and mental sanity.

I was an unwanted child, born in South America, which has a colonial mentality and is run by a Macho Society. Both of my parents were sociopaths and managed to sell a respectable image to the world as they were high profile in their own right. My relatives in close proximity always had passive aggressive behavior. They wanted me to suffer and would happily go out of their way to make my existence as miserable as possible. They would not do anything to benefit me, even if it didn't cost them a penny, and that is not an understatement.

During a beach vacation, I think I was about six-years-old, I almost drowned due to negligence from an aunt who pleasantly looked the other way as I was getting sucked into a change of tide. The person rescuing me reported the incident to my mother and nothing was done about it.

When I was a teenager, my father left me and my mother destitute in the middle of the Christmas Season without a full dollar to buy basic groceries. As a result, I hated my life every time December came around. It was so bad that I earned the nickname Mrs. Grinch! (Side note, I recently changed that!).

The week of my birthday in 2017, my mother left without a trace, taking my valuables, cash (while I was financially struggling), and important documents. In addition, I was the one responsible for $63,000 in debt which I am still paying on. Due to her crafty work, inconsiderate actions, and despicable behavior, I bled about one half million dollars - and then some due to interest accrued- personal belongings, and priceless time and energy along the way to ensure her immigration to the U.S.A. Yet, I continued absorbing the obligation to be the savior in every crisis, regardless of poor decisions made.

I was a slave to unreasonable cultural expectations that almost took me to the graveyard. I never had the clear guidance showing me that I should protect myself -even from those blood relations- at all times and at all levels; mentally, emotionally, financially, and physically, without feeling guilty about it. I hope you put these pearls of wisdom to good use for your own sake and safety!

I have endured so many extended stays in Hell, yet miraculously those situations didn't get the best of me. I managed the unmanageable thanks to, what I call, **"The Power One;"** the one person willing to help during a crisis, bend reality for me, or the one thing I could do (depending on my available resources) to stay away from fully losing myself. Whether it was a quiet day at the museum, taking a dance class, or doing extreme sports, I allocated time and funds for my personal version of self-care, even if I had to keep it as a clandestine operation. By leveraging my talents with curiosity, creativity, and resourcefulness, I was not only able to take my craft internationally while breaking records at the professional level as an independent artist, but also led me to discover my very personalized Holy Grail!

You might be skeptically asking what's that fuss about? After so many trials and errors in the quest for a prosperous living, decades of ongoing mental and emotional abuse, and rising above my version of PTSD, I decided to cut the bullshit out of my life. I took a peaceful holistic approach by using Ikebana (The Japanese soothing art of floral design) as a regular therapeutic activity intertwined with neuroscience to properly mitigate my environmental and mental chaos. I started to develop a program around the topic. I named it **"From Chaos To Calmness"** and I'm on a mission to share it with the world because of the amazing, life changing results I've experienced and I have an absolute faith that similar and greater outcomes can be attained by many when provided with the right guidance and structure.

Not only is it a healthy way of self-expression, but also an outlet to process emotions, grief, and painful losses. It's a means to create a conducive Zen space for productivity and high performance. Because this has become my new lifestyle, my creativity is unfettered, intuition and problem-solving skills are off the charts. Inner peace has become a reality rather than feeling as if it's unattainable. I have learned to celebrate accomplishments in a very intimate fashion by getting in tune with my surroundings. And most importantly, I've become a master in delivering smiles.

If you can relate to my experiences in any way, I can assure you that going on a quest to find your own Holy Grail will evict you from the hamster wheel. The easiest way to start is by finding a passion and make it a priority, a non-negotiable, cultivate the right environment that is conducive to its flourishing, and watch the magic happen! You might even find stardom like I did.

Before this moment of bonding comes to an end, I want to lovingly thank you for your time -as this is the one resource you can never get back- and extend an invitation for us to stay in touch. I find a handwritten letter, mailed the old fashion way, to be a very charming act and a dying art. So here is my address. I am eager to read how you find your own Holy Grail!

P.O. Box # 31; Arlington, Massachusetts 02476; USA

Meanwhile, I encourage you to rock your own style and choose happiness, right here, right now! These are the good old days! Make them count!

With much appreciation and ever blooming creativity, I am rooting for all your talents and ever-growing list of accomplishments! (In all sizes! Big and small!)

Nefertiti San Miguel
Queen of Bloomtopia

P.S. Do more of what you love, less of what you tolerate, and none of what you hate.

WEBSITE: **https://etniafusion.com/**

YOUTUBE: **https://youtube.com/user/EtniaFusion**

FACEBOOK: **https://www.facebook.com/Etnia-Fusion-by-Nefertiti-120992106966/**

https://www.facebook.com/nefertiti.freytes

Nefertiti San Miguel

PAMELA MORGAN

To Taija-Rai

My heartbeat, my inspiration, you continue to teach me that living in a state of grace is within reach - you just need to believe.

PIVOTAL MEMORIES

by *Pamela Morgan*

We all have a story, and our stories consist of a multitude of memories. For many of us, our memories are safely tucked away and ready to make a debut whenever one of our senses is awoken and, depending on that recollection, the entire orchestra of senses will take front and center and the film reel can begin to play. Let's be honest, that picture show can bring up all the feelings, even the ones that hang in the shadows that we prefer not to talk about.

This is my story—my memories, should I be blessed enough to remember them. Hopefully my experience can help those who are building memories of their own.

My mom passed away from dementia three years ago. During the last five years of her life, her memories would just slip away quietly. It appeared that, through divine intervention, only the memories that caused her sorrow and pain disappeared. She could no longer remember the loss of three children—two of them from murder and a daughter to SIDS. All the struggles that life had brought her, poof, they were all gone.

In my naivety, it seemed like she was given this final gift from the divine to prepare her for the other side. And in my grief, before and after she left this world, I reflected back on my own life, as we do when someone we love is leaving and our mortality becomes very real. I had the slightest amount of envy over the possibility that I could someday forget my own traumas, my sorrows, and my pain accumulated throughout my time here on earth. However, I also recognized that sometimes our painful memories—the memories of those pivotal moments, sometimes seconds, that forever change our lives—are worth remembering, because without them we wouldn't be who we are today.

This is one of those pivotal moments for me.

It was Christmas Eve, 1990, and I was finishing my shift at the café, serving the last round of coffee to the nightshift staff. My abusive ex-husband had told me a couple days prior exactly how he was going to kill me, in explicit detail, and that I wouldn't see Christmas Day. That was one of the rushes I think got him off—fantasizing about how he would be there as I took my last breath. His promise was one hundred and twenty-six stab wounds to the chest, and "The next time your family hears about you, it will be on the six o'clock news."

A couple police officers were on their usual rounds that evening, and I served them. One of the officers was a regular at the café, but I'd also had the misfortune of being introduced to him when I had called the police a couple months earlier when my estranged husband had slashed my tires, leaving his version of a "love letter" to remind me *No one will ever love you like I do.*

In my call to the officer, I'd told him what happened and, before I could finish, he told me he knew who slashed my tires, as the police were very familiar with my ex. I was tired and scared—and I had been for basically the entirety of our eight-year relationship. I'd met my ex when I was only a child myself at fifteen. I was exhausted, and now I had a little human to protect—a baby daughter. I wanted to get out, hopefully alive, for both our sakes.

So, I asked the officer, "What can we do?"

He'd replied, "Well, we can go over and talk to him. But I'll be honest, the next time I see you, I'll be zipping up a body bag."

So, that was my answer. All my fears had become a reality. I'd hidden in an abusive marriage for years, and no one knew because of the shame and fear. At that moment, when the officer had shared his thoughts, it confirmed all my fears for me. Remember when I was speaking about memories? Well, my memories were alive. Throw in some childhood trauma, and I was firmly reminded: "No one is coming to save you. You are on your own."

My daughter was staying with my ex's parents over Christmas—my way of extending an olive branch and trying to keep the peace. When you have endured a volatile and abusive environment, you become an expert at people pleasing and making things appear normal.

When I got home from the café that Christmas Eve, with my ex's threats and the officer's words in my head, I knew I wouldn't see Christmas. I wrote my final goodbyes to my daughter, family, and best friend. I placed the letters in my hope chest, knowing eventually they would be found. I lay back in bed and waited for my ex's prophecy to begin. I said a final prayer, pleading that my daughter somehow would be safe, and I eventually fell asleep.

On Christmas morning, to my shock, I woke up. I was alive. Nothing articulated my feelings better than these words (author unknown):

> *"The most beautiful music in the world is your own heartbeat; it assures you that you will survive, even when it appears the whole world has abandoned you."*

That was my pivotal moment, the moment I woke up on a day I never expected to see, and my life was forever changed. I know this sounds extreme, but I'd felt I'd beaten death. Well, at least I had been granted the opportunity to rewrite my story, my future.

It was a new day, and I thought, "Okay, you're being given this second chance, girl. You better start fucking showing up for it."

Now let's be real, I didn't suddenly throw on my superwoman cape and take to the skies, fight crime, and protect the innocent. The very first and only priority I had was protecting my two-year-old daughter from becoming a statistic. The writing had been on the wall that she would eventually become collateral, as I had been, whether that was for personal pleasure, for his friends, or for people he owned money or drugs to. I may not have known who I was or where I was going, nor did I have the strength or desire to save myself, but by God, my daughter was not going to be a victim in this world. (For the record, she saved me one hundred percent, not the other way around.)

For me, this was the key to the kingdom: PURPOSE. It took years and is an ongoing practice of self-awareness, standing in my truth, forgiving myself, and forgiving others, but I took my experiences of abuse, addictions, grief, and mental illness, and I found a purpose in them. Now, decades later, I have the honour of serving others in multiple facets as a founder of a non-profit charity, as a coach and mentor, and in my HR firm. Because we all deserve a chance at a better life—and sometimes we deserve second and third chances, too.

Everyone has a story. Our stories consist of multitudes of memories and some of those memories are riddled with trauma. My story isn't unique, but my experiences were, because of how I reacted and how it molded me in the light and in the shadows. My memories are mine alone, and because of how they shaped me, I wouldn't ever want to lose them—even the bad ones. You, your story, and your experiences are intimate to you as well. We need to remember we each have this immense power, a silent warrior inside us all that is waiting to rise up and change the storyline, overcome, realize our resilience, and begin again even when we feel broken.

I have always struggled with the word *broken*—especially in relation to the human experience. "She is broken," and "His life is broken" feels so final to me, unrepairable. No one is broken. We need to stop devaluing ourselves. Our words become truth. As hard as it is to hear, we can either be a victim, or we can be victorious. We can sit, dwell, and surrender, or we can rise up, stand in our truth, heal through helping others, and rewrite our stories.

We may be battered or bruised through this thing called life, but those scars are unique to each of us in creating the masterpieces we all become. It's through our grit and grace that we become warriors. My wish for all of us is to be brave, step forward, start a new chapter, change the storyline, and take back our power.

Pamela Morgan

WEBSITE: **www.keyinsctincts.com**
www.bcocharity.com

FACEBOOK: **https://www.facebook.com/KeyInstincts**
https://www.facebook.com/babyitscoldoutsideyyc

LINKEDIN: **https://www.linkedin.com/company/key-instincts**
https://www.linkedin.com/company/baby-it-s-cold-outside-charity

Pamela Morgan

RACHEL RIDEOUT

I would like to dedicate this chapter to my grandson, Jonathan. Because of you I strive to make a better life for you and myself every day. I hope that I can instill in you, values of hope, imagination and knowing you are loved every day and truly worthy of all that life has to offer. My Monster, I love you!

~NawNaw

CHOOSING A LIFE WORTH LIVING FOR

by *Rachel Rideout*

I was tired. I was so fucking tired! Tired of being miserable every day. Tired of being treated like a worthless piece of shit by everyone around me. I had flunked my college courses. Every day at work I was harassed, bullied, or lied about to my supervisors. It was so bad that I would literally pray on the way to work for something bad to happen and hurt me so I wouldn't have to go to that living hell anymore.

My own child was stealing from me, fighting with me, physically and mentally almost on a daily basis. My grandson and I would have to walk on eggshells around her because we didn't know what would set her off. She was trapped in a drug addiction and refused to admit she had a problem. Pair this with what I believe she had was mental health issues and you have a cluster fuck of a shit storm I was dealing with on a daily basis.

I had no safe haven. I couldn't go to work and escape the rampage at home. And I couldn't go home and have a safe place to be myself, be at peace and not have to worry about anything. It seems my whole life I have been the one for people to blame and put forth their anger, rage, hate and bitterness. My last intimate relationship my partner was very narcissistic, one day I was the best person on the planet, the next I was the reason for all his problems. If I got upset with this it was my own insecurities and selfishness that was the problem, not him. Having to sit for hours and listen to him talk about himself, if I interjected or tried to share my own thoughts, I was rude and selfish.

Friendships were ending, people I had been friends with since childhood turned their backs on me. The time when you need your friends the most, they left me high and dry. They didn't care about what I was going through in my personal life or at work. I learned through this trial not to trust anyone and I was on my own. I had no one and nowhere to go. I still to this day have trust issues and it is hard for me to make friends because I feel I cannot be my true self around anyone.

So, there I was sitting on my bathroom floor having a total mental breakdown. I had the bottle of wine in one hand and a mixture of pills in the other. I just wanted to go to sleep and never wake up. At least this way it would be peaceful and maybe I would wake up in a heavenly dimension where there truly is peace and love.

This wasn't the first time I had considered taking my life. I remember as early as 11 years old writing suicide notes, only to hide or throw them away. Maybe I was too chicken shit to actually off myself or maybe the universe had bigger plans for me I was unaware of and that is why I never followed through? But, on that day sitting on the floor, my daughter and grandson had come home. I heard my grandsons sweet little voice calling for me, so excited to be home and to see me. I couldn't leave him here to fend for himself with all the crap my daughter was putting this baby boy through. I had to stay here and protect him!

I made a decision that day to turn my life around. I had to do something to stop this cycle and to not allow anyone to hurt me anymore.

That night I began listening to meditation videos on YouTube. Every evening as I was going to bed I picked a video that I felt I needed to help me with whatever I was dealing with that day. Videos for confidence, music for healing. Tibetan healing bowls are truly one of my favorites to listen to. I AM affirmations became a daily mantra for me. I even created my own prayer for protection which I believe has truly helped me when I need it most and I still use to this day.

I truly believe what you speak out loud to the universe is what you will attract. Once I learned about journaling and how writing things down on a piece of paper and then speaking them out loud to the universe, everything started to come together.

Sitting at my desk, lighting candles, listening to music or writing in complete peace is sacred to me and one of my favorite ways to end my day. Healing my inner child, the one that was hurt by bullies, men touching me and my father who mysteriously disappeared, the girl who every relationship told her she was not good enough.

My inner gifts have begun to manifest and I have realized I am an empath who is here to help and guide people who have been on a similar journey as mine. The more I become in tune with this gift the more intense it gets. I can read energies, which can be a good and bad thing. The good part is I have learned who is for me and who is actually against me. If your energy is off, I will avoid you like the plague. Negative energies really eat into me,

I am still learning how to block those negative vibes so they do not affect me so intensely.

Life will never be easy, but it doesn't have to be so hard. I think we as people tend to make life hard on ourselves. Worrying too much about what other people think and allowing society standards to dictate who or what we should be. I still battle with depression, anxiety and feelings of being worthy and good enough. The techniques I use definitely help me in those times.

Working on yourself should be a never-ending process, I figure if you stop then you're dead. We all should be striving to be better people every day. Our planet has enough negative bullshit going around, decide to be a ray of sunshine and hope for yourself and the people around you. Challenges will always arise, these trials in our lives mold us into who we become and we as people have a choice to do good or bad with it. Life is all about choices and you can choose to take those things that have made you a victim, you have the power to refuse to let it keep beating you down, take complete control and come out victorious!

There is a life worth living and you are worthy.

Rachel Rideout

RUBY LEE MCDONALD

In honor of Melba W. McDonald, a woman whose life embodied the definition of the word "mother". Thank you for adopting and raising this stray.

GOD'S GIFT OF LOSS

by *Ruby Lee McDonald*

It took losing my mom for me to find myself.

What kind of monstrous person thinks something like this?! I guess that would be me, and I have some explaining to do. My mother was an angel on Earth, I would not even be alive if not for her, but it took her death for me to find myself – who I was meant to be.

My mom, Melba, was not my biological mom, but she was the epitome of motherhood. This paragon of a woman raised two sets of children that were not hers biologically. During her first marriage, she experienced a miscarriage at seven months, losing her only biological child, Michael. Her second marriage was into a ready-made family with children ages 1, 2, and 3, with full custody. She stepped into that challenge without hesitation. One of those stepchildren was my biological mother, Susan.

Susan was not able to be a full-time mother, nor provide a safe environment, through no fault of her own. She was born with a brain tumor. At six weeks of age, a surgeon tried to remove it but half a century ago technology was not as advanced as it is now. Despite his best efforts the doctor's knife slipped and cut into her brain casing. She became mentally challenged. Due to this, when she became pregnant with me, she was not deemed safe to raise me alone. My biological sperm donor is a story for another time. That drama could have launched me onto a pole for a career if I had been skinny enough.

Enter in Melba, technically ex step-grandmother, who had divorced my biological grandfather after 19 years of marriage and helping raise three stepchildren as her own. Don't worry if this family tree starts getting weird, I feel it makes some extra branches and U-turns, but as confusing as it was, it is one of the greatest blessings of my life. Now at this point in life, Melba was on marriage number three, in its first year. She was 53 years-old and was imagining in a few years what retirement would look like for herself and her spouse. A phone call in the middle of her work shift would destroy all those dreams. No one was really able to explain how they got hold of Melba at her job, except it was a miracle. She was high enough up in the BellSouth company that someone recognized her name and found out which office she worked at and got the call patched through.

A NICU nurse from Jacksonville was desperately trying to reach out to find next of kin. Thanks to what can only be described as divine intervention, she able to reach Melba at the office. Melba was told she had to come to Jacksonville by midnight that night to pick me up from the hospital or I would be turned over to the state and put in the system. If you think DCF is a mess and struggling now, imagine what it was like 40 years ago before the internet existed. Melba was in shock, she explained she didn't have a car seat or anything to accommodate a newborn. The nurse said that she would gather some things and that Melba should just start driving up to the hospital. Melba prayed about it and told her husband that she was going to pick me up and take me home. She would rather have his support to help raise me but would still take me in without his help. There is a reason I called her "mom" and him "grandpa" my whole life, much to the confusion of most people.

This 53-year-old, newly-wed woman raced to the hospital to rescue me from a life of being in the foster care system. The nurse had made a cardboard box with some hospital blankets and told Melba that she would turn her back and ignore the fact that she had no car seat type of device. With this, I was sent home like a stray kitten found in the street. My mom always laughed while telling this part of the story of how I was smuggled home. She continued to work until I was in middle school before retiring after almost 50 years with BellSouth. Most people imagine their retirement as vacations, travel, fine dining, golfing, etc. My mom's retirement was PTA, chaperoning field trips, school nurse, the designer and creator of Christmas show costumes, and so much more. She was at every soccer game, every night of a show I performed in, I was truly blessed to have a parent that was able to be active in my life. She gave up her retirement to raise me. Then because of a health issue, I was able to pay that gift back to her.

My mom had a heart attack that resulted in a quadruple bypass surgery on Christmas Eve. Melba being a strong, fierce, and independent woman passed those traits on to me. The miracle God gave me for having an older parent raise me, was that because she was retired, she was able to be there for me. I am who I am today because of how she raised me by her example. Now I was 17 and she needed help. I would be able to give back to her what she gave up for me.

I had several full ride scholarships to great universities, but I gave them up to go to Daytona Beach Community College. A secret I kept from her for decades. By being home while taking classes, I was able to take care of her as she recovered and got stronger. There was never an ounce of resentment or feeling of toddler-like tantrums that life was unfair. After all, she gave up her life to raise me from scratch, it was my turn to give that love and commitment back to her. Fast forward through college, med school, and my own marriage, my mom would need me again.

I knew my husband was "the one" when he stayed by my side during an emergency heart surgery for my mom while we were just friends. As they wheeled her into surgery, he turned to me and said that it was ok for me to "turn off", I had been strong long enough it was ok to let go and cry, to feel. He was the first person to ever give me permission to not have to be on top of everything. I ugly cried into his shoulder ruining his shirt. He had no clue what that conversation did for me; I knew I was never letting him go. Mike has been the rock, the partner, the best friend, and soul mate I prayed to God to have in my life. My mom knew he was the one because I shared my food with him, growing up an only child, I never learned to share well, especially delicious food.

A year into our marriage, five months in our new home, my mom had to have another heart surgery with a pacemaker. This is not the ideal situation newlyweds look forward to when all of the sudden your mom is going to live with you indefinitely, in fact I am sure there are sitcoms about the horror stories of this dynamic. We were blessed that it was a wonderful situation and worked out without any daytime tv like drama. Mike got to spend time with her and learn about my upbringing firsthand. My mom gained a son-in-law who had the same name as her son. I am so thankful that God gave us this time together. A few months later I was injured with a traumatic brain injury and my mom and husband were there to help me through it. Things went downhill for my mom shortly after. She began showing signs of dementia and we tried everything to help slow it down. There is nothing more heartbreaking and soul crushing watching your loved one slowly leave you one piece at a time.

I slowly lost my mom in pieces, but throughout her four-year battle with dementia, God used it to help me find myself and purpose. This amazing woman who raised two generations of children, not hers by blood, made me who I am today. Through losing her, I found myself, my purpose, and my strength to become the determined, independent woman who knows her worth and will never settle for less. I try my best to make her proud by being able to help other people while showing the love that was given to me. Melba brought people together, even as she was at a memory care facility, she brought amazing relationships into our lives. Her legacy will live on in the lives she has touched, and in mine as I continue to serve others.

If you would like to connect with me, please find me at:
https://linktr.ee/rubyleemcdonald

STACEY ROI

I would like to dedicate this chapter to the Father, the Son and the Holy Spirit. Without God's amazing grace and mercy, I would never have come to know how powerful His endless love is for us all. Thank you for taking me on this incredible journey and saving my life. Amen.

PING!

by *Stacey Roi*

It began as any Facebook friend request does. A ping from your phone, a little icon of two people and a number next to the icon indicating your pending friend requests. It beckons to you. Wanting you to click on it to see who is on the other side. Who has noticed you? It's almost hypnotic what it does to people, but not this girl. I'm all business. The no nonsense type. The one who rules her phone, not the other way around.

After a few minutes, curiosity got the best of me. I had three requests waiting. I had held out long enough to not be under the power of that notification beep! Without a second thought and in a manner that was automatic, ingrained in my brain, my finger swiped the top of my phone screen downward and touched the notification from Facebook. Ahhh, the excitement you feel when you don't know who is waiting for you to respond.

As I have always done with any friendship request, due to the nature of my networking business, I accepted all three. However, one, in particular, really caught me off guard and seemed to stir a fire in my soul. It was a fire that, at the time, I was unaware of the magnitude that would soon engulf me at my core and change my life forever.

After all, it was just a profile picture. One of a very handsome man sitting in what I assumed was his kitchen, working on his laptop at the bar top counter with a cute little Yorkie dog sitting on the high bar stool next to him. It was a striking picture. Elegant and fine. I am not sure why it spoke to me so deeply, mesmerizing me as I studied every detail from the flooring to the lighting over this tall, dark, Italian stranger who wanted to be my friend. "Oh well," I thought to myself, "maybe he'll be interested in my business, and I will have a new contact in San Francisco, CA! That would be a nice place to build a team."

Until now, I had never paid much attention to friendship requests, other than checking some of their pictures, since pictures are worth a thousand words, and where they live and perhaps if they had any mutual friends. This man, known as Alexander Hill, was different from all the others I had received before. He had a new profile and no friends and just a few pictures of himself dressed for business, in cities overseas, working out in his home gym, him in front of an elegant car and him traveling on a private jet. Intriguing, nonetheless.

What was it about him? His stunning good looks? His soulful blue eyes set off against his dark brown hair? I didn't dwell too long, but I did think to myself that there wasn't something quite right about Alexander Hill. He was cute, but hey, I was married for 17 years to my husband, and we had been together for 23 years. I never really looked at another man. I was focused on my family and my business. No distractions because all distractions are equal. Never take your eyes off the prize. That was me. Focused, unshakeable, immovable, loyal, honest to a fault and happy with my life...or so I thought.

I closed my computer and didn't give another thought to my new friends, but what I didn't know was that lightning had struck me in the darkest place of my soul and started a smoldering fire that would soon grow to an unquenchable inferno...

Hello, my name is Stacey Roi, and I was a victim of an online romance scam. I can assure you, first of all, that I am not the "normal" person you think would be fooled by such a con. I was a successful businesswoman, running a networking company with my husband of 17 years (together for 23 years). We had three daughters between us and what looked like the perfect American family. I wasn't even aware of the bomb that was ready to explode our world. It is hard for me to believe the journey I went on because everything was so out of alignment with me. It wasn't who I was. I felt like I was watching myself from above and it was truly unbelievable. I am sure that I was under a spell since I could not help myself when this man invaded my life.

I recall thinking am I really going to do this and walk away from everything I have built? My marriage, my daughter, my step-daughters, my family, my life, all my material possessions and security to go be with a man whom I knew was a con man? The answer was, yes, because we actually fell in love with one another or something like that. It was such a compelling, driving force that even a stubborn, strong-willed girl like me could not fight. I felt powerless.

I told no one where I was. I didn't tell anyone I was divorced, including my family. I felt so much shame and embarrassment. I wanted to hide from the world until I could come to my senses. Unbeknownst to me at the time, I was on a life altering journey that there was no escape from. I had to go through it and either die along the way or emerge victorious. I left the country for the first time in my life at age 51 and settled in a foreign land where no one knew my name or the man I was with.

It was quite the adventure and I lost so much, but I gained everything. How, you ask? I lost my 'fake' self only to find the real me. I lost money in the form of cash and four houses, but I gained something greater than material possessions. I learned who I truly am, the daughter of the Most High and Powerful God. I lost my prejudices and preconceived notions and found compassion and empathy. I lost what I thought was happiness and gained true joy. I lost self-hatred and learned to love me. I lost fear and found peace. I lost my life and found everlasting life in Jesus.

I worked feverishly on personal growth. I experienced various stages of death, yet I was more alive than ever before. I felt like I was a wild mustang running for my life trying to escape from something pursuing me, caged in by towering canyon walls on either side of me with only a dead end ahead. The sky was so blue above me, and I would always look to the Heavens. I kept running and growing closer to God. He was all I had for those five years.

It was a journey of a lifetime but devastating. I passed through Hell to emerge out the other side like the Phoenix rising from the ashes. It's not something one should have to go through, and it is very detrimental to the person, their family, and friends. I am here to help those who have been victims of these horrific scammers to regain hope and their life and prevent others from becoming victims by teaching them the signature signs of these tricksters.

If you would like to connect with me to discuss things in greater depth or if you just need someone who will simply listen to your story and not judge you in any way, please don't hesitate to reach out to me.

You can schedule a complimentary chat with me at **https://calendly.com/staceyroi** or reach me via email at **contact@staceyroi.com**. Please visit my website at **www.staceyroi.com** and I will send you my free eBook titled, *"10 Signs that it is a Romance Scam."* Look for my story coming soon!

May God bless and keep you safe.

ACKNOWLEDGMENTS

What I have found as the Founder of *The Victim to Victory Podcast*, is that **Change starts with our story**. Finding our true voice and stepping unapologetically into our own wonderful authenticity.

I encourage and challenge you, To wear your story like a superhero cape and not an anchor. Much love to my family, Ray, Cheyanne & Abbey, for helping me break generational trauma to leave a legacy of love & empathy for generations to come.

My most grateful thanks and respect for all the Authors that are the Visionaries of tomorrow, lighting the way for many others.

ABOUT THE PRODUCER

Tracey Cook

Tracey Cook has every reason to not be a success. Living a lifetime of trauma, Tracey tells and shares stories that inspire and create transformations. She gives the audience the direction into transformation to find their purpose, step into their story, and find their voice.

ıtning Source UK Ltd.
ɔn Keynes UK
W021556050123
85UK00018BA/259

9 798986 781761